Directing
in the Theatre
Second edition

Hugh Morrison

A & C Black · London
Theatre Arts Books/Routledge · New York

The cover photo, by Nobby Clarke, is reproduced by courtesy of the Royal Shakespeare Company, and shows a rehearsal of *King Lear*, which opened at Stratford upon Avon in 1982, directed by Adrian Noble.

From left to right: Sara Kestelman, Jonathan Hyde, David Bradley, Jenny Agutter, Adrian Noble, Christine Kavanagh, Ray Llewellyn, Clive Wood.

Second edition 1984
Reprinted 1989 (revised bibliography)

A & C Black (Publishers) Limited
35 Bedford Row, London WC1R 4JH

Second edition by A & C Black 1984

Published simultaneously in the USA by
Theatre Arts Books
an imprint of Routledge, Chapman & Hall, Inc.
29 West 35th Street,
New York,
NY 10001

First published by Pitman Publishing Ltd 1973
First published in paperback 1978

UK ISBN 0–7136–2596–1
US ISBN 0–87830–587–4

© Hugh Morrison, 1984, 1973

Printed and bound in Great Britain
at The Bath Press, Avon

Contents

I
The Director's Job

Tyrone Guthrie said that if you want to learn to direct plays you must find any group of actors willing to let you direct them and get on with producing a play. This process must be repeated, with success and failure, many times, and the would-be director must learn from it. Many good books exist which explain the arts and skills of acting, directing, and the technical crafts of the theatre: they are a vitally useful aid to the director, as a manual is to a mechanic, but in no way a substitute for practical experience. Such books are a summary of know-how, a consensus of opinions on the ways in which different people approach the task and of their aims and methods of working. The object of this book is to examine the function of the director in practical terms, and to explore in some detail the creative aspect of the work.

The contemporary director enjoys a position of both power and prestige. Some directors are so popular and influential that their name alone can draw audiences by the polish, originality, or skill of their work; some are known to be masters of a particular type of play, others to be exciting in their handling of a wide variety of work, from classical revivals to new plays with stimulating subjects and experimental form. The director of today is credited with the talents of a creative artist, and with being no mere organizer of actors and scenery but someone who puts the play through an imaginative process. The object of this creative project goes far beyond arrangement of resources. It is to give the play a life on the stage that the written text cannot possess: to enhance its virtues, disguise its faults and limitations, and to help a company of actors to clothe it with meaning and feeling, which exist only as an idea till expressed by the performers. The potentialities of the job have never been greater; the director is a twentieth-century creation, an artist-cum-executive who has evolved out of the need of the modern theatre.

The theatre of the present day draws heavily on the traditions of the past, and the director now fills all the roles that have been undertaken in previous generations and cultures by an assortment of people, dramatists, actor managers, stage managers, and even high priests. The theatre director cannot ignore the experience of centuries: he must have an awareness, knowledge, and sympathy for the theatres, plays, actors, and audiences of past ages. Nothing dates so quickly as fashion, modes of expression, the texture of everyday life: the theatre is ephemeral, and deals with the transitoriness of life, yet we constantly return to those plays which survive time, because they contain unchanging philosophical truths about the nature of mankind, whether expressed through the medium of tragedy or comedy. The theatre must relate to life, be fresh and pertinent, and those who work in it must be sensitive to changes in art and life, and not create monuments to dead art and aesthetics. Theatre consists of re-running those bits of human life we want to see again, either to enjoy them anew, reaffirm our beliefs, or simply to understand: it can only be enjoyed if the right means are chosen to convey the experience. Audiences are growing more sophisticated, with the ability to compare and judge both the matter and the manner of a play and to recognize the form in which human experience is presented. We no longer need the scrupulous scenic realism of the Victorian actor managers who literally demonstrated every locale in a play with elaborate effects, yet we can appreciate their desire for theatrical splendour combined with truthfulness to the dramatist. Similarly we understand the motives of William Poel, who reconstructed a stage similar to Shakespeare's: his attempt to make the plays work in terms of speed and use of space has influenced every modern director of the Elizabethan classics.

The History of the Director

In previous times, control of the rehearsals of a play might be held by the writer, as far apart as Sophocles and Shaw. Or in the age of early scenic theatre by a combination of poet and scenic artist, if the poet was Jonson and the artist Inigo Jones. Shakespeare and his principal actors and managerial partners probably shared the responsibility for mounting his plays and advising the actors. During the nineteenth century the actual organization of rehearsal and performance was in the charge of the prompter or stage manager, who kept the prompt copy containing details of moves, business, and the operation of scenery and effects. All these functionaries exercised their authority with their own particular bias: the dramatist toward the exposition of story, the scenic artist toward the provision of spectacle, costume and dance, the prompter toward rigidity of performance where actors were hardly rehearsed at all, and acting was determined more by established custom than the needs of spontaneous reality. The quality of acting, by which every performance stands or falls, has mainly been dictated throughout the centuries by great or good actors, of talent and experience, understanding the conventions of the theatre of their time, and the expectations of audiences. And if the drama of the time was healthy, who better than the actor to decide how the audience was to be regaled?

The advent of modern naturalism at the end of the nineteenth century brought the director into being. The spontaneity of the play with realistic dialogue and stage action, and freedom from conventional or stylized expressions of fact or feeling, made the evolution of performance an exploration, rather than an exhibition. Leading actors were too concerned with the demands of their roles to conduct such unpredictable rehearsals, and an outsider became necessary to help in evoking performances, characters, relationships and the overall meaning of the play. Naturalism connoted a greater reality of writing and acting, and changed the audience's enjoyment from mere pleasure at the virtuosity of a few actors to a more balanced appreciation of the play and its characters. So the modern director's first function was to transform virtual solos into part of an orchestrated work.

Theatres of the past were conventional structures. The very buildings and their architecture had for the audience meanings which were widely understood: in the theatre of Euripides, part of the stage represented the royal palace, the exit to one side led to the town, that to the other side to the country. The chorus, singing, speaking, dancing and miming in their circular arena were an understood link between play and audience, able to switch between being detached commentators and involved characters. The theatre of the Elizabethans used no scenery beyond the stage itself, which provided a number of acting areas: the outer apron, the inner stage, and the platform above the inner stage. Scenic spectacle was contrived by groupings of richly dressed actors, and the audience readily accepted the realistic limitations of entrances and grouping: for example, important speeches to a large number of characters might be delivered from the upper stage. The experience was visually unreal, except in the physical relationship of character to character, and effects were produced from the roof over the stage, or a trapdoor underfoot. A god or a devil could only rely on the effectiveness of his appearance and the power and skill of his performance. The audience supplied the rest with their imagination. Within the limitations of such conventions as these, the possibilities for stage action were restricted: no lighting, no scenery, a convention of significant gesture and rhetorical practice, even in the case of the Greek tragedies a predictable sequence of scenes in the play, made the director as we now understand him superfluous.

When choice of scenic effect, flexibility and realism of action, spontaneity of speech demanded an arranger and arbiter, the prototype of the modern director came into being, and his influence and responsibility has increased ever since; it is unthinkable that a play should be presented without having been first interpreted and then realized by the director.

Variety in Directing

Now that we have the control of the production, in all its aspects, in the hands of one person, we must examine what his responsibilities are and the varied circumstances in which he may be called upon to work. It is necessary to generalize and state that there is good, bad, and mediocre direction, as there is more obviously good, bad and mediocre acting; however, poor direction is often difficult to identify, and may be redeemed by play and acting, and excellent direction may pass unnoticed. The quality of the end product is not infallibly related to professional status, long experience, a big budget, or an intellectual approach to the business of directing. Many exciting productions start with inexperienced actors, an ill-equipped building and no money for lighting, scenery, and costumes. The same principles of analysis, organization, and handling of actors and technicians must be applied to the business of directing, whether it's a £250,000 West End or Broadway production or a school play. Only a few directors have the opportunity to work on the highest level, with consistently fine actors, good plays, and unlimited resources of money and talent. Whilst they have a responsibility to maintain an output of achievement which is never less than superb, this does not mean that the rest of the theatre from repertory in the provinces to the thousands of amateur theatres, should think in terms of substandard theatre. Shortage of finance and lack of facilities is used too often as an excuse for lack of application and real desire to serve the audience: the ingredients of good theatre can be boiled down to good acting, the product of deep thought and hard work, and good material, judiciously chosen. All the rest, attractive buildings, technical resources, publicity, restaurants and bars, are the wrapping round the package, and tend to be overemphasized as a means of attracting and keeping the loyalty of the public.

The talent for acting and directing, and doing it well, is much more widespread than is generally believed, but tends to be undeveloped because of the belief that theatre should be treated in a dilettante fashion: that to do it well is a sign of presumption, and will be NO FUN for audience or actors. The circumstances of theatre are very diverse, and most professional directors will be called upon to work in widely varying conditions: from directing untrained amateurs or schoolchildren, or teaching and directing professional drama students, to working in relatively luxurious conditions with good facilities and highly skilled professional actors. The key to a satisfactory result in all these cases seems to be an ability to maintain the vision of what the end product is going to be, yet to change emphasis and reorganize the priorities of directing. The play must finally work on its own terms, whatever method is used to achieve performance.

The successful director of a good company of amateurs needs to be able to rehearse over a period of perhaps four weeks or three months, often in the evenings only, with part-time unpaid actors, yet he must maintain and demand a standard of work which compares satisfactorily with the professional theatre. In many places the little theatre or amateur groups are solely responsible for providing entertainment for thousands of people. Such a director has a very diversified role, sometimes working with actors of skill and talent, sometimes teaching the ABC of acting to beginners; given that he is a capable and imaginative director, he needs the specific skill of making his rehearsal work cohere into a production when rehearsals are fragmentary, and abilities very varied. The personal qualities of such an artist are all-important as he has no authority as an employer and there is no financial reward for the actors.

The professional director working in a provincial playhouse has different priorities and problems. His actors and staff will be trained, talented, and dedicated; and probably in the first years of their professional life, so against all odds he has a responsibility to continue their training and help their development as artists. Rehearsal time will usually be too little, with overworked and underpaid actors cast beyond the range of their abilities: the mature and experienced actor who works in the provincial theatre usually does so for the chance of extending his or her talents, by playing challenging major roles. They are entitled to sympathetic and skilful direction, rather than being expected to bear the burden of the success of the production. Where time is such a limitation, the greatest artistic problem is producing a fresh, spontaneous, truly creative result, not letting himself or his actors fall back on mere expertise, clichés of acting and production—the hoary old pro attitude of "just say the lines and don't bump into the furniture." The occasional director of a company of novice actors is faced with the basic problem of inducing *any* acting, let alone presenting an interpretation of the play. He will probably have to teach an entire cast to use their imagination and observation, and concentrate on the rudiments of effective acting, economy, audibility, repose, and meaning. Subtleties and the finer points of the play are a waste of effort if the basic needs haven't been fulfilled. Two roles for the director begin to emerge: the interpreter of the play and the trainer and guide of the actors. Where very talented and experienced actors are gathered together for a production, the director's job may be to provide a framework of planning and organization, and a few main points of interpretation: acting not as a trainer, but as an audience, a sounding-board, and an organizer of creative ideas. The highly gifted actor, amateur or professional, can't be taught to act, he can only be helped to discover and evolve his performance, and to relate it to the play in the best possible way.

The very differing circumstances of directing are further complicated by the nature of the plays and dramatic material. The ability to pick plays that please the public must be combined with a keen sense of values. Any one play must be part of an overall programme, which aims to present the widest possible range of entertainment and stimulus, yet it must use the actors available to the best of their abilities. The paying public cannot be expected to tolerate either monotony of fare because certain plays suit the actors, nor ghastly mistakes where the actor learns his trade all too obviously in public. Certain plays seem to need a completely different type of actor, but this is only partly true. It is a widespread assumption that actors with little ability or experience can satisfy an audience with a thoroughly commercial comedy or thriller because it appears to be "lifelike" yet must not presume to muck about with *Uncle Vanya* or *Hamlet*. The latter plays, because of their innate qualities of truth about life, experiences and the behaviour of mankind, will use the most valuable quality the inexperienced actor posesses: his humanity. The out-and-out commercial play demands great expertise and confidence: being quite possibly trite and shallow, it needs actors who can make the obvious and the banal fascinating, who can bring charm of personality to two-dimensional characters. Here the star actors come into their own, and many years spent perfecting their one role are rewarded. The success of such plays is more dependent on good casting than on good direction. With the right actors, a distinguished designer capable of making the actors and the settings look beautiful, the director's job appears easy: yet the one essential requirement may be that he acts as a link between the actors, or supplies some emotional need which feeds their creativeness. Miss X, who is very good value, may only produce results for someone sympathetic who admires her beauty and personality; Mr Y may only be funny for someone who agrees with and appreciates his unique sense of humour. Obviously directors should aim for the versatility of interest and ability that is demanded of the contemporary actor, and be able to handle a wide range of material, and be helpful to actors of very differing ability and status. A director cannot expect satisfaction or reward if he confines himself exclusively to one type of play. This means risks must be taken and new skills and approaches learned throughout a career of directing.

The responsibilities and duties of directing are time-consuming. Every director should be economical about the amount of work he has to do, and this involves delegation wherever possible, as in any job of management, leadership and policy-making. The director must gather round him the right sort of associates, which may involve knowing not only a considerable number of actors but also technicians in every department of theatre: technicians capable of making decisions at a high level, and exercising artistic sense and creative talent. It is important that he can get on with the business of directing, supported by a flow of work and ideas. There are few professions where the boss's job is so ill defined, and too many productions are marred by the directorial assumption of the head-cook-and-bottlewasher role, most notably in the amateur theatre. Creative thinking, calm observation of the actor in his struggles is impossible if the director is encumbered with routine tasks. An experienced practical assistant with authority and organizing ability is of more use to a director than the occasional services of a few brilliant actors. Only in the last few years has the job of theatre technicians been put on an equal footing with acting, and we are beginning to realize how valuable their contribution is. For decades productions staggered on poorly served by man and girl Fridays, in the same slapdash tradition as the acting; "They're only amateurs" or "It's only the rep."

The minimum staff of technicians to a production would seem to be a general stage manager, plus two assistants: a designer/craftsman, embracing scenery and costume, preferably with workshop skill; a chief electrician with an interest in lighting design, and a secretary. Through the ages, the artist of the theatre has bravely borne extra tasks, and working conditions which no other skilled worker would tolerate, on the assumption that if he didn't, his theatre, his authors, his job and his public would disappear. With increasing leisure, and the growing complexity of life the place of the theatre in society is being redefined. In a form that is still evolving it is more necessary than ever in the cultural desert, and its practitioners must organize themselves to cope with the demand for theatre, and realize that the satisfaction of the artist can be combined with the skill of the craftsman and the business sense of the trader.

The Director as Artist

Having considered the variety and responsibility of the director's job, let us try to discover the core of his work. The success of his efforts will be finally judged by the quality of the acting and the plays he presents, and his direction may pass unnoticed by the audience, whatever interpretative skill, brilliant teaching, or organization he may have contributed to the corporate effort. It is an old truism that if a play succeeds the actors get the credit, and if it fails the director gets the blame. This may be so, but at least the director can nurse his failure in private and does not have to run the gauntlet of a hostile audience. However, as the modern theatre becomes more adventurous in its techniques and subject matter, so the work of the director becomes more apparent. The greater intellectuality, the decline of theatre as a sentimental two-hour wallow has sharpened the audience's appreciation of the ways and means employed to divert them. Obviously the first and foremost part of the director's role is as midwife to good acting. This involves being at best a connoisseur of acting, and expert in its techniques, and at worst recognizing the phenomenon of good acting when it occurs, and making encouraging noises in the hope that it will go on occurring. He must be aware of the exercise of acting skills, and able to demonstrate his points. A director who is not excited by acting is a theoretician who will be bored by rehearsal, and convey that indifference to the actors. This does not mean that the director must have the performing skills and stamina of the actor. A director who can act his cast off the stage, or who wants to, is not likely to inspire confidence in the actor who is trying to solve the equation between what he is and what he's got to act. Understanding of the process and technique of the actor, emotional, physical and intellectual: skill in the use of voice and speech, and the technique of applied movement, and a knowledge of how these skills apply to actors of all ages and types, gives the director something to offer to the actor as positive, constructive help.

The examination of the role, and of the actor playing it seems to be such an exacting task as to preclude any possibility of the director being involved as an actor: even our great actors, some of whom are also excellent directors, produce less than the best when trying to work in this double capacity. It seems essential that the director's view of the characters should be detached, without involvement in the anxieties and ambitions which are to do with the characters as roles, as vehicles for acting. From the director's standpoint, acting seems a narrow but intensely concentrated art, concerned with just about everything, but demanding precise skills of expression: the actor should possess the capacity to express more than he knows: to express everything. The help the actor needs in the creation of a character seems to be of several kinds: first, elucidation, discussion; discovering the nature of the character, and relating it to the situation and the other characters; next, advice about the means, how it is to be realized and conveyed: how spoken, how moved, how the emotions are to be used. As we have become liberated from conventions of theatre, and predictable forms of expression, so the method has become more eclectic: whatever works, and conveys feeling and meaning can be used—a great dilemma of style for the actor. The actor needs help as an individual, above all encouragement and sympathy; he needs to understand his limitations and weaknesses, and his powers, of intelligence and emotion; also his relationship to other actors. It seems facile to imply that the director should be a sort of Universal Aunt to the actor, but while not professing to be a psychologist he must be a friend. This last form of help is given all too little under the pressures of the profession where competitiveness keeps down the price of actors. The actor who is not a thick-skinned pro may be regarded as a professional incompetent. The demand to deliver the goods or else may blunt the very sensibilities that make acting good, or kill the delicacy or sensitivity for ever. Good acting cannot be induced by logic and rationality alone.

The Director as Interpreter

The other main task of the director is to interpret the play according to the dramatist's intentions. For many directors this is a more congenial job than the trials, the friction, the sheer repetitiousness of rehearsals. It seems to offer some chance of conceiving a personal vision of a play, which the actors can then be asked to realize in acted terms. Certainly somebody must be able to take an overall view of the meaning, the means and the effect of the play—somebody who is free of all other responsibilities, either artistic or technical. This raises the question of whether the director should have great technical grasp of the machinery of theatre. If it can be combined with detachment from the attraction of presentation for its own sake, the conception of how to stage the play should stem from the director: only a knowledge of lighting, stage setting, costume, and effects can translate a concept into a reality. Actors demand the security of an efficient staging, however simple, a decision about the style and convention to be observed, and to know why the play was written. In trying to understand the basic intention of a play, to convey it to his actors, the director may discover possibilities which depart fundamentally from the dramatist's ideas. It is a great temptation to want to be seen to have taken an interpretative standpoint, to make the intellectual work of directing noticeable to everyone by challenging the obvious conception of the play. Preparation by the director should be so leisurely that the bees in his bonnet have flown by the time he starts rehearsal, or orders scenery, so that he is aware of a wide variety of possibilities of meaning and effect, yet is open to the further illumination of the text and characters that should arise in the course of rehearsal.

To direct is to sit in the hot seat: to spend other people's money and time. Circumstances are seldom ideal, so the director must be a fanatic, a dedicated enthusiast, to be prepared to shape the amorphous mass that is a play and actors before production. Only a methodical approach, allied to a free and liberated imagination can produce a result. The desire is not enough.

Supporting any successful production is a mass of work which may have started months before rehearsals. John Dexter, before staging *A Woman Killed with Kindness* at the National Theatre, had been ruminating on the play for many years. It is possible to get a play on in ten days from first having read the script, but the obvious risks are shallowness of conception, or misunderstanding the meaning of the play, and slapdash acting. Under pressure, actors and directors tend to resort to clichés of performance, generalizations and over-simplified meanings, even plagiarism of other actors' work; it's funny, but sad, that so many actors should have spent years giving their No. 1, No. 2, or No. 3

performance! So the director tends to repeat what's worked before in a comedy, regardless of a different text and totally different actors. Patience with himself is the first need of a director, the nerve to wait for creative ideas, and the courage not to act upon the first idea that comes into his head.

The Director as Manager

At this early thinking stage of planning, organizing capacity is called for. A director must develop a healthy capacity as a businessman, with a sense of the connection between art and profit. The work must be properly co-ordinated so that skill and time are properly used: this capacity is especially necessary in the director who is running a company or a theatre. However, whether one production or one of a programme of productions, the questions are the same. Can the play draw, and interest an audience? A theatre can only afford to stage a just proportion of experimental or controversial plays, unless it has an established reputation and following as an *avant-garde* theatre. Policy would appear to be the ability to please the public while broadening their minds, increasing their acceptance of new materials and new methods. Will the budget allow for staging necessities? Does the play need expensive settings and costumes? Are suitable actors and technicians to hand, even if the play is going to extend them? Often in quite respectable circumstances productions are mounted regardless of the suitability of the actors, who are disappointed by the public reaction to a brave try. Is the theatre or hall or market-place suitable, or adaptable to the needs of the play? The conventional theatre building is no longer a *sine qua non*. Most important, do I like the play, can I see its virtues, have I a good reason for directing it? The professional director has little freedom of choice if he wants to earn a living, and the amateur director a much greater freedom which he seldom exercises.

Personality and Experience

What sort of person, then, makes a theatre director? Obviously many types of people manage to adapt themselves to a job so multifarious. It would appear that a gregarious, opinionated power-mad extrovert would fill the bill: certainly ambition and the desire to be boss must play a large part. The reality is that

ambition must be above the desire for personal success, yet someone who shrinks from power and influence and responsibility will
be largely ineffectual. A wish to entertain and communicate is
vital. A director must be a relentless publicist, even when a publicity manager's services are available: public enthusiasm for
theatre is often tepid, and all the enthusiasm that can be generated
is necessary to ensure an audience. P.R. is more than a connection with the local press that ensures tolerant notices, it is the
theatre director's constant relationship with the audience, and
his interest in the life of the community which comes to see his
productions, whether it is a village, a university, or a huge in-
dustrial city. Self-discipline and ruthlessness are necessary, without
which creative talent can't flourish; the director must be able
to cut a play and sack an actor if the end product is likely to be
impaired. Yet the director must never lose sight of the fact that
when a play goes into performance his work is done. The dramatist wrote it, and the actors bring it to life. The director without
humility and a resilient sense of humour cannot induce creativeness in others, or indeed in himself. Many directors are actors,
or have been actors, and the experience as a performer gives
them delight in good acting, no matter who is giving it: to assist
in the blending of a number of fine performances is surely the
most rewarding experience in the theatre. Love of dramatic
literature is essential, though it must not be divorced from the
facts of performance: no play when acted can live up to the
nebulous ideal performance which exists in the director's imagination. Creativeness and scholarship exist in a very delicate relationship. The truths revealed by a good piece of theatre cannot be
stimulated by pedantically intellectualizing the play. The scholar
invariably supplies everything the artist wants to know about a
play, except how to act it. The popular picture of the theatre
director as all-purpose intellectual is impossible to live up to.
True, he must be intelligent, deductive, reflective, curious, and
rational, but there are times when logic and intellectualization
can get in the way of intuition, and the director's creative thinking
and human sympathy can dry up, making rehearsal a dull
business for the actors. A typical example is the long peroration
before a first reading or rehearsal, when all the possibilities of the
play are given a four-hour dissection. During the first hour the

actor is mentally muttering "Well, that's not what I thought it was about," or he is alarmed that he has seen so little of the true import of the play. Often we theorize to avoid the painful discovery that nothing is happening, that we must struggle for a long time to understand, let alone to create. From what actors say about their rehearsal experiences the two most important factors of fruitful direction would appear to be understanding and sympathy and clear expression of ideas.

Previous experience of the theatre, of whatever nature, is useful. The actor-director will bring to directing a knowledge of the ways and means of acting, the technical and emotional problems; technicians, designers, stage managers will bring organization and method. Perhaps the ideal director is someone with a passionate interest in acting, plays, and the creative process that leads to performance, yet with no desire to take an active part in stage managing, acting, or designing: a finger in every pie, overall responsibility for the artistic quality, yet bearing none of the burdens of the individual tasks; something of a dramatist, something of an actor, something of a technician. Whatever balance of these qualities exists in the director, they cannot be put to use without a particular attitude to the work: insatiable and broadminded curiosity, love of mankind (and actors in particular), sensitivity to his surroundings in all their social, human, and political fluctuations, indefatigable energy and enthusiasm. In the final analysis, the director seems to be the editor and presenter of human beings: of their lives and their joys and their sufferings.

Few arts are subject to as much theorizing as the theatre: perhaps that is its fascination. The theory of production, however well one understands it, however admirable the philosophy of the director, does not get plays on to the stage. In the following chapters we will try to follow the practical process of the work, using examples from particular plays, and consider the use of speech and movement, the analysis of the text, the role of the technician, and the fundamentals of production.

2

The Analysis of the

fundamental de
ship. It is po
and actors
With
a be

The analysis of the play the direct
hearsals will powerfully influence th
for worse. He will formulate certai
and effect of the play and its charac   ...aru to
abandon during rehearsal, when several other minds and personalities are possibly in conflict with his ideas. His private
meditations may seem the only time when he is personally creating
something, even if it's only a dreamlike phantasmagoria of events
and images. It is a vexed question how much the play should
be prepared, and the realization preconceived. Preparation may
mean that like a good general the director has a plan of action,
knows his resources, and is aware of the possibilities existing in
the play; or it may mean that he has no more than a few hunches
and cannot clarify his ideas till the play is in rehearsal. If we are
to conclude anything about the right amount of preparation
beforehand, it is that in most circumstances actors and director
alike benefit from an organized framework, but that mulling too
deeply over the text can lead to fixed ideas about the means and
meaning of the play. Peter Hall said recently that ideally the
designer of a production should attend rehearsal, and as the
production evolved so should the environment, costumes, and
physical conditions surrounding the characters. Peter Brook,
directing Seneca's *Oedipus*, allowed the actor's mode of dress
to arise out of discussion and awareness of the needs of the play.
Hall has also said that blocking, that is the pattern of movement
and action, should develop from the necessities and motives of
the characters, in the process of examining the text. Both directors
are here thinking of an ideal way of working, with unlimited time
and perfectly trained actors. Most directors would prefer to enter
rehearsal with the moral support of a few clear ideas about the
general nature of the play: the mood and tempo, the bustle or
stillness of the action, the nature and effect of the speech, the

...ils about the characters and their interrelation-
...sible to take a starting point and develop from it,
...are reassured by the confidence of the director.

...increasing experience, the director becomes more assured:
...tter judge of his own response to the pressures of rehearsal
...id of the actor's creativeness, and also of his capacity for
organizing the happenings of a play in a coherent and theatrical
way. The more his experience, the greater his pure skill as a technician. Put not so elaborately, this means a flair for guessing what
the actor's getting at, and a lot of know-how about theatrical
effectiveness. There is an obvious danger in not doing any home-
work—loss of the actor's confidence, and chaotic rehearsal. In
our pursuit of spontaneity and freshness we must not ask too
much of the actor unless we know him very well, and the improvising director is liable to be taken for a lazy director. Well-
thought-out possibilities are the director's salvation when nothing
happens during rehearsal, when performances don't develop;
alternatives are there to be pursued, and the director doesn't have
to hustle the play into some kind of shape, often using the very
tricks and clichés he sought to avoid in the first place.

Advance Thinking: Text Analysis

There are many considerations bearing on the director's advance
preparation. The experience and talent of the cast dictates how
best to use rehearsal time, and their way of working must be
found out as soon as possible. Apposite casting saves time, and
many circumstances dictate that the director can't take risks.
Time and money may determine the style of presentation.

All begins with the director's first reading of the play. This
should be rapid and alert: the director must try to put himself in
the position of the audience, who will only hear the dialogue
once. It is very difficult, but essential, that he returns again and
again to this realistic audience view of the play: the production
is for them, not for the participants. From this reading he will get
an impression which will be very like their impression, whether
the play is strong in plot and action, or rich in character development, and whether the language has any particular quality of
poetry, imagery, or humour: whether the play is visually spectacular, or simple and unadorned. He must be able to judge what

combination of qualities makes the play effective, but need not possess the capacity to pass instant judgement. Wherever possible, a project should be nursed for as long as possible in advance. The director seeks for any means to enrich the texture of the play, and clarify its meaning. This may mean jotting down ideas as they occur: these are the spontaneous notions that cannot be summoned at will, particularly under the pressure of rehearsal. The director amasses ideas as a writer collects material, and like the writer tries to organize them into some sort of coherence before rehearsing. These random ideas may come from any source: from life, with the director basing characters on people within his own experience; from art, music, literature, history. Nothing at this stage can be discounted. A production must have a starting point, like the actor's performance, which may be as nebulous as the weather in a particular scene, or the clothes worn by one of the characters.

The director's knowledge of the text is at first slightly awesome to the actor, but invaluable at a later stage of rehearsal. It enables the director to get his nose out of the book, and watch what his actors are doing. The director of a production was once dismissed simply because he did not do this: his ideas were admirable, his handling of the mechanics excellent, but unfortunately his actors thought he was oblivious to their efforts! Reading and analysis should extend to knowing the order of scenes very clearly, the content of each part of the play, and finally a great deal of the dialogue, as a conductor might know the score of a symphony. Obviously this familiarity with the text must not imply a rigid approach to its interpretation. The director must be receptive and flexible enough to change his ideas if necessary as the play melts under the impact of the actors, and their experience and intuition. Much of the text may be revealed as rehearsals progress: only familiarity with the lines allows meaning to arise. Many directors and actors will have found that true meanings of lines, or how to express them, or the real nature of a situation occur to them after many performances, often years later when returning to a play!

Text analysis falls into two areas: the play itself, its form and meaning, and secondly the technical and artistic necessities, in terms of presentation and actors. It is difficult to take a long view of a play in the light of one's own preferences and prejudices. How does it say what it means? This is the basic directorial decision. A clear distinction must be made between form (the how) and content (the what). So the play must be viewed first of all as a structure—a progression of dramatic action, events affecting its characters. These may be outwardly circumstantial, as in the whodunnit, or a hard-to-define general situation, with an emphasis that may be political, social, moral or spiritual. Such is the limbo of Beckett's *Waiting for Godot*, with Vladimir and Estragon locked in a general dilemma: to go on, to nowhere; to make away with themselves; or to await the long-protracted coming of Godot—a symbolic situation, used as a vehicle for philosophizing, exploring emotion, hope, human relations, and a multitude of other human possibilities.

The plays of Chekhov contain little ramification of plot. Such events as occur are often spread over a long time-scale, for example the impending sale of the cherry orchard. There are few happenings that directly affect the lives of the characters, as for example the death of Tusenbach in a pointless duel, which occurs at the end of *The Three Sisters*. The mainspring of the play is the presence of a military garrison in the town where the Prozorovs live, and the relation between some of the officers and the family. In *Uncle Vanya* Vanya staggers through his middle life, absurdly innocent: for him and Sonya the important event of the play is that they should go through a crisis of disillusionment: Vanya has worked and toiled to support the greedy Serebriakov, and discovers him to be a fraud and a louse on the locks of art, Sonya has longed for love and marriage, and sees the inevitability of spinsterhood awaiting her. Together they face disappointment, and a bleak future.

By contrast with Chekhov, the plays of Shakespeare abound in plot and action. *Hamlet* contains a complex of interrelated action: the motivation of Hamlet through the appearance of his ghostly father and his plot to have revenge on Claudius; the counter-plot by Claudius to remove Hamlet to England. The two main plots produce much subsidiary action: the destruction of the relationship between Hamlet and Ophelia, leading to her death; the death of her father and brother; the employment of spies, the enactment of past crimes by a troupe of actors, the miniature drama of Hamlet and Gertrude, the threat of military pressure from Fortinbras, finally the last act of murderous revenge—what Claudius intends to be a disguised assassination rebounding upon him. Plot here is clearly of great importance, and its unravelling gives the play its tension and dramatic effect. Yet plot can sometimes be a mere vehicle on which to hang frivolities or satire, as in the comedy of manners. In *The Importance of being Earnest*, the question of whether Jack and Algy will acquire suitable names, and woo Gwendolen and Cecily to the point of marrying them is merely a means to the delicious end of revealing the characters in their world—how they converse, live, love, and enjoy themselves. Here the emphasis is hardly even on character, charming though they are, but on the expression of an idea of character. The comedies of Ben Jonson use plot as an expression of an idea of great importance: the possession of enormous wealth, or the possibility of possessing it, and its effect on certain types of character, with comic exploitation of their folly. The balance between plot and character is difficult to understand, and actors and directors are constantly redefining it, seeking and finding new relevance to life and thought, submerged motives: as, for example, Professor Kott's analysis of the cyclic nature of power in Shakespeare's histories. Sometimes the dramatist scrutinizes life just to see its texture, sometimes human motives, institutions, philosophies, and habits. Some plays have a verbal quality of a high order: poetic language, exquisite literacy, profound cogency: sometimes the form is realistic, spare and down to earth. Yet we cannot say that Shakespeare is a better dramatist than Brecht, Ibsen than Shaw. The difference for the director is one of dramatic means, not quality.

The text of a play is finally to be acted, and the only proper criterion of a dramatist is the playing of his work. Let us consider two plays for the purpose of analysis of form and content, and technical and artistic needs. The object of this examination is not to state categorically how they should be directed or staged but to see what sort of ruminations are likely to lead to results.

" The Birthday Party ": Form and Content

Pinter's fascinating play defies analysis at the first reading, in spite of appearing to contain many elements of powerful theatricality. A reading reveals amusing characters, comic dialogue, hideous and tragic metamorphosis, tension, dramatic irony, unity and progression. It seems to belong to the genre known as Theatre of the Absurd. In terms of content, a tremendous but unexplained event takes place: the furtive slob Stanley Webber is discovered living as a petted lodger, almost a member of the family, in Meg Poole's boarding house. Goldberg and McCann impose themselves on Meg "for a short holiday." They contrive a birthday party for Stan, though it isn't his birthday. Before and during the party they threaten, bully, and coerce him; accuse him of innumerable crimes, sins and failings, treat him violently and reduce him to a state of mindless, cowed idiocy. They then take him away to receive the probably worse attentions of "Monty." So Stan has been transposed from peaceful, cosseted idleness to a fate worse than death. Yet it is never revealed why this awful and seemingly probable chain of events takes place. Who is Stan, and what has he done? He is accused variously of murdering his wife, leaving The Organization, picking his nose, and watering the wicket at Melbourne. Who are Goldberg and McCann? What legal, moral or social authority do they represent, and what right have they to commit monstrous acts upon the life, body, and mind of another man? Either the play is a hoax, a brilliant piece of joke Grand Guignol, or it's seriously meant. Certainly, the Orwellian central idea of nebulous guilt and punishment looms as a very pertinent metaphor of an aspect of modern life, though perhaps Pinter himself would not claim such a serious intent. The other characters in the play, Meg, her husband Petey, and the sexpot neighbour Lulu, are excluded from Goldberg and McCann's designs, and are peripheral to the events: they are there to be acted upon, to be used, conned, seduced, and made unknowing accomplices in the destruction of Stanley. Yet they are much more than mere tools of the plot, and have tremendous life and vitality of their own, and qualities of comedy and pathos. The first reaction is to think that one must abandon all ideas of making a factual construe of why the events come about, to satisfy the audience's desire for a rational explanation. These things, we must say, simply happen, and there are many parallels in life of cruel inhuman destructiveness in the cause of ideology, morality, and loyalty. Our present awareness that it can and does happen seems to be all that matters immediately. No attempt is made to draw conclusions about the rights or wrongs, whether the punishment is deserved or whether it fits the crime. So we are compelled to consider the form of the play, to see what it reveals. In spite of the horror of its implications, it is very funny indeed. The humour comes from several sources. The characters' use of language has a certain unity of style, what John Mortimer has described as "Ruislip Mandarin". As most of them are apparently lying most of the time, the point is made about the difference between expression and intent. The use of language is also justified by the fact that they are pushed to the extreme point, mental and social, of their characteristic state: they are to some extent, exaggerations. Goldberg is a mythomaniac stage Jew, whose main stock-in-trade is his talk: he sells false *bonhomie*, shopkeeper values, middle-class morality and bourgeois nostalgia in a brilliant flood of hyperbole and rhetoric. This is saved from unreality by the fierce intensity and energy of the character, and his humour: he can laugh at himself while boasting of success, and expounding the idealized suburban life.

Meg at first appearance is a stock figure, a traditionally comic seaside landlady, crass, gullible and dotty: a lampoon from a music-hall sketch. Yet she is much more, and arouses complex emotions. Flirtatious, complacent, and pathetic, she is another character who uses myth: the myth of her happy childhood, her desirability, her abilities as a housewife and as a proprietress. Though her motives for lying, exaggerating, and distorting the truth are pathetically self-justifying, as opposed to the cloudy and savage ones of Goldberg and McCann, she must use the language of deception none the less: language is used as a stylistic device which shows how honesty gets lost and truth may disappear in opaqueness.

MEG. My little room was pink. I had a pink carpet and pink curtains, and I had musical boxes all over the room. And they played me to sleep. And my father was a very big doctor. That's why I never had any complaints. I was cared for, and I had little sisters and brothers in other rooms, all different colours.

Lulu and Petey are very close to reality in their dialogue, though

Lulu has some nice moments of pulp fiction when reproaching Goldberg for her seduction.

LULU. .... you quenched your ugly thirst. You taught me things
a girl shouldn't know till she's been married at least three
times! ... You didn't appreciate me for myself. You took
all those liberties only to satisfy your appetite. Oh Nat, why
did you do it?

McCann is very much a stage Irishman. Pugnacious and hard-drinking, narrow and puritanical, he apes Goldberg, while providing the contrast to Goldberg's smoothness and charm. Stan himself appears to have much to conceal about his past, and resorts to fantasy and lying. His sole weapon of offence and defence seems to be slangy cant and pomposity:

STAN. I had a unique touch. Absolutely unique. They came up to
me. They came up to me and said they were grateful.
Champagne we had that night, the lot. (*He pauses.*) My
father nearly came down to hear me—well, I dropped him
a card, anyway. But I don't think he could make it. No, I—
I lost the address, that was it. (*He pauses.*) Yes. Lower
Edmonton. Then after that, do you know what they did?
They carved me up. Carved me up. It was all arranged, it
was all worked out. My next concert. Somewhere else it
was. In winter. I went down there to play. Then when I got
there the hall was closed, the place was shuttered up, not
even a caretaker. They'd locked it up. (*He removes his
glasses and wipes them on his pyjama jacket.*) A fast one.
They'd pulled a fast one, I'd like to know who was responsible for that. (*Bitterly.*) All right Jack, I can take a tip.
They want me to crawl down on my bended knees. Well, I
can take take a tip any day of the week. (*He replaces his
glasses and looks at Meg.*) You're just an old piece of rock
cake, aren't you? That's what you are, aren't you?

Hilarious stuff, but there's more to it. Pinter has arranged their cliché-ridden speech most artfully: figures of speech, platitudes and spurious maxims abound ("Breathe in, breathe out, take a chance, let yourself go, what can you lose?"). The form has nearly become the content: their talk is what they are.

The problem for the director is to create a reality from speech which appears at first sight naturalistic, but is often carefully edited into rhythmic patterns:

GOLDBERG.   Why did you never get married?
McCANN.   She was waiting at the porch.
GOLDB.   You skedaddled from the wedding.
McC.   You left her in the lurch.

It begins to appear that the acting priority of the play is vocal, since the dialogue is so complex. There is much action, some realistic, some ritualistic. Meg, when drunk, dances an absurd solo waltz: McCann when bored tears a newspaper into regular and exact strips with the concentration of a fanatic. A game of Blind Man's Buff is played, a child's game turned to a ritual of torture and persecution, with the sweating and panic-striken Stanley as the victim. However, much of the play has the outward appearance of domestic comedy-drama. On what level of reality is it to be treated? Symbolism would seem to be heavy-handed and portentous: the dramatist himself at one stage refused to attribute "meaning" to it, on either the realistic or allegorical level. The characterization is highly individual, richly idiosyncratic, yet they are pasteboard figures: an Englishman, an Irishman, and a Jew; a landlady, an old man, and a young girl. They have no clearly explained past, few deep expressions of self-awareness, and seldom tell the truth. It is in the vivid articulation of their limited ideas, their narrow feelings, that they come to life. A picture emerges of the sort of actors that the play needs. They must be well cast as to type, but this is not enough: comic actors, with abilities verging on playing comedians' roles in the case of Meg and Goldberg, who are both "Cards" in their own estimation: serious actors, but not romantic actors. Above all they must possess fine vocal sensibility, with considerable flexibility of voice and speech, who can appreciate the form in which the play has been written and the characters realized. When this demand has been satisfied we have room for manoeuvre in terms of personality, temperament and appearance: Meg may be tall or short, Goldberg fat or thin. The actor playing a large role in a realistic small-cast play bears a great burden of credibility.

To throw more light on the characters, for purposes of casting, we must look further into the total effect of the play. Meg, for example, is a woman of staggering banality: she says hardly anything precise, or even intelligent: she has a very small vocabulary, and a total lack of refined qualities, and the general effect is asinine and pathetic. What can we assume to counterbalance these negative qualities? First, she must be comic in herself, in her personality and appearance: there is an implicit contrast between her soppy romanticism, genteel ceremoniousness and deplorable appearance, and her energy, gaiety, and powerful emotions. She would be a very sad figure if not armed invincibly against fate by the smallest of wants and an infinite capacity for self-deception: "I was the belle of the ball. Oh yes. They all said I was. Oh, it's true. I was. I know I was."

Goldberg appears as a figure of cynical ruthlessness and fatuous values: "a little Austin, tea in Fullers, a library book from Boots and I'm satisfied," yet he is neither villain nor buffoon. He is immensely engaging: his virtues are intellect-proof, and we must want to lend him ten pounds against our better judgement. The instrument of his power is his charm, energy and magnetism, and an eloquence that enables him to turn platitudes into something dangerously close to originality and feeling, and to transmute corn into humour. He must surely possess the ability to amuse not only the credulous Meg but the audience too, and to invest the man without qualities with the mantle of a leader. One might surmise that his clothes are as meticulous as his manners, and that the poet of the dog stadium also acts the self-mocking role of the Jewish comedian.

So the process of reflecting on the characters' possibilities must continue in depth before casting: what sort of actors, in terms of special abilities, personality and looks. The naturalism of the play, the apparently stereotyped characters, seem to demand recognizability of looks and voice. If naturalism is the acting medium, the play seems to need an appropriate staging, and the dramatist suggests a realistic setting. Realism in design in this case need not connote pedantic re-creation of a tatty boarding-house living-room, but the capturing of its atmosphere, claustrophobic and comically squalid. The play makes few technical demands, except that it shall be lit in accordance with the mood of the scenes. The nature of the action does not make it dependent on a proscenium theatre: it could equally effectively be presented on an open-end stage or in the round: the late Stephen Joseph demonstrated a most effective in-the-round setting for this play.

To summarize these few reflections, the director must accept without reservation the unexplained motivations of the characters, and seek to exploit fully the fascinating verbal forms of the play; he must cast with meticulous care, and stage with an eye to a realistic impression.

A Classic Tragedy: Form and Content

Let us now consider a very different type of play: a large-cast non-naturalistic costume play, with the added complexity of poetic language—*The White Devil*, a powerful, spectacular Jacobean tragedy by John Webster. As this is a book for directors, and therefore enthusiasts, the chosen examples are of plays that are the best of their kind, but many of the same problems of staging, organizing, and performing will occur in a large-cast romantic musical! The big sweeping drama is something that belongs particularly to the theatre and is less satisfactorily presented on Television, which presents the human face in close-up to particularly good effect, but minimizes and trivializes the big ensemble scene.

The first impression is of enormousness, as with most of the tragedies of the Elizabethan and Jacobean period: enormous cast, many scenes and locales, language full of imagery, terrific deeds, opulent and powerful people. In these very qualities lies its fascination: it's a rich canvas, full of feeling and action, yet its plot suggests not a look back into a long-dead past, but a contemporary reality. A brief résumé of its thematic ideas will confirm this. First, the ruthless exercise of power, temporal and spiritual: Brachiano has offended the Duke of Florence: to pursue his passion for Vittoria Corombona, he has murdered his wife, Florence's sister, and Vittoria's husband, the cousin of the powerful Cardinal Monticelso. He has defied them both, and Florence sets out not only to crush him, but to humiliate and torment him. Next, opportunism versus poverty: Vittoria and her scheming brother Flamineo are from a virtuous but poor family; both of them are clever and attractive, but these qualities combined with virtue will bring no reward in a world where power and wealth and aristocracy are the only recognized qualification for supremacy. Vittoria must use her beauty, Flamineo his wits: they must prostitute themselves to passion if they are to live above the level of humbleness and poverty. Next, the fallacy of inordinate love, of the sacrifice of principles, scruples and humanity to Eros: for love, or lust, Brachiano, Vittoria, Flamineo die.

The play presents many technical problems: a large cast and many scenes. The sheer numbers of actors are reducible by intelligent doubling of roles, with the proviso that the small parts, as indeed in any worthwhile play, need good actors to fill them. The many locations of the play could be provided by the use of either a composite setting or an imitation of an Elizabethan stage for which the play was written. The play is very long, and consequently must move rapidly, without scenic encumbrance, so the provision of various acting areas is necessary for fluidity: yet the play is Italianate, classical, not Gothic in feeling, and a reproduction of the Elizabethan playhouse might seem quaintly archaic to a modern audience. The various scenes abound in visual, pictorial possibilities. There are nine scenes which might be daylight, six night, and several of a highly theatrical atmosphere: assignations, murders in dumb-show, a trial of a beautiful woman, a Papal procession, a scene of armed sports, a couple of ghost scenes, a scene of madness, and a macabre tableau of death and torture. At this point lighting resources seem of the utmost importance, but we can take heart by remembering that the first audiences enjoyed the play without artificial lighting. It would seem that the play needs full and artistic lighting, or the simplest: its effects and moods are strong, and inadequate and "arty" lighting would detract from its power. Costuming the play would be expensive, and where possible should be simplified: most of the characters require only one basic costume, in some cases with additions of hat and cloak, but Vittoria needs several changes, as her dress is commented upon in her trial scene, as being inappropriate to widowhood. However simply the production is staged, the realistic weapons will be needed, and a fight arranger to create the fight at barriers—a specialized sort of contest, and spectacular and dangerous. Actors should not be instructed to go away and mug something up: every thirty seconds of a fight sequence needs many hours of rehearsal, for both safety and verisimilitude. Similarly, the scenes of dumb-show are a convention of theatre and may need special instruction in mime. Because of the formal nature of some of the action and the frequent changes of scene, it would seem practical to devise exits, entrances, and groupings in advance.

The many visual effects possible or necessary make illumination a priority. Much admirable work is done in presenting the spectacular play, or opera or musical, which is then spoiled by too little light of the wrong colour. Historicism is not an absolute necessity, however, and there are alternative possibilities in presenting the play out of an Elizabethan context, though updating costume should never be used as a mere gimmick: it often appears to be a gesture of no confidence in the play itself or a fear that the audience will be bored. This text, in quality of language, character, and dramatic events, seems fascinating, given good acting, speaking and production. Even in the bleak atmosphere of the rehearsal room the power and excitement of the play comes across. If any attempt is made to modernize the presentation, it must be done with great subtlety, to preserve the effect of the characters: that is, how their clothes reveal their power, status and sex appeal. The nearest thing to Vittoria we can produce in our society is a film star on the make: could she be dressed like one? Might Brachiano or Francisco dress in sumptuous uniforms, like contemporary military dictators? Probably such a transposition would be even more expensive than period costume: mink and good tailoring!

The play needs music. The text suggests a song and a certain amount of ceremonial music, and the drama of these scenes can be heightened by its use. The linking by music of fast-moving episodes is also effective in sustaining atmosphere. What music? Some years ago Clifford Williams, discussing the use of music in plays, made the point that using it for its own sake made it superfluous. Worse than too much music is music that has associations for the audience which are irrelevant to the play. Even allowing suitability of period, and appropriateness, familiar music has emotional connotations which are different for each member of the audience. So any music that is used should ideally be created for the play. This would seem to be a tall order, yet there are many talented amateur musicians capable of creating original music and performing it. The pop music industry wouldn't exist without such people, and they're worth looking for. Obviously a background in classical music helps, preferably with own synthesizer! The essence of theatre music is that it should be simple and effective, so a feeling for the emotional, the popular and the atmospheric is important, as is a talent for pastiche. If it's to be done by professional musicians, it's going to be expensive. If original music is unobtainable, proprietary recordings, and unfamiliar music should be sought.

In spite of the formidable technical requirements of the play, we must not lose sight of the strength and quality of the text: as a more trivial and light-hearted entertainment like a romantic musical might founder without highly decorative presentation, so this play will perform with good acting and direction only. A group of actors in practice clothing, with a bare stage, and a minimum of props and rehearsal furniture, can convey the play to an audience's total satisfaction. A naturalistic play, concerned with tangible everyday realities like the cut of a woman's dress, cucumber sandwiches on a plate, would be marred by simplified presentation.

Guthrie, in his last pronouncements after a lifetime in the theatre, opined that speech was the actor's medium. This skill is even more obviously required in this verse play, where imagery, vivid metaphor, and rhythm supply for the audience all the realism that any amount of theatricality cannot supply. As St Denis says, "The text has its own power, it creates its own meaning." Consider these examples:

MONTICELSO.   Shall I expound whore to you? Sure I shall;
              Ile give their perfect character. They are first,
              Sweetmeats that rot the eater; in man's nostrill
              Poisoned perfumes. They are coosning Alcumy,
              Shipwrackes in calmest weather. What are whores?
              Cold Russian winters, that appear so barren,
              As if that nature had forgot the spring.
              They are the trew materiall fire of Hell,
              Worse than those tributes i' th' Low Countries payed,

Exactions upon meat, drink, garments, sleepe,
Aye, even on man's perdition, his sin. . . .

VITTORIA. Dye with those pills in your most cursed mawe
Should bring you health, or while you sit o' th
Bench
Let your owne spittle choake you. . . .
Instruct me some good horse leech to speak Treason,
For since you cannot take my life for deeds,
Take it for wordes—O woman's poor revenge
Which dwells but in the tongue—I will not weepe,
No I do scorne to call up one poore teare
To fawn on your injustice—beare me hence,
Unto this house of—what's your mitigating Title?

MONT. Of convertites.

VIT. It shal not be a house of convertites—
My minde shal make it honester to mee
Than the Popes Pallace, and more peaceable
Than thy soule, though thou art a Cardinall—
Know this, and let it somewhat raise your spite,
Through darknesse diamonds spread their ritchest
light.

BRACHIANO. Your beautie! O, ten thousand curses on 't.
How long have I beheld the devil in chrystall!
Thou hast led me, like an heathen sacrifice,
With musicke, and with fatall yokes of flowers
To my eternall ruine. Woman to man
Is either a God or a wolfe.

However much actors may bring to these roles in terms of creative imagination, to act them satisfactorily needs commensurate
vocal technique: a rapid and agile articulation, subtle and
flexible rhythmic sense, good breathing and the ability to sustain
tone. So much work will have to be done on the speaking of the
text, not only from the standpoint of interpretation, but technically, to ensure that the meanings intrinsic in the form are conveyed: the vibrancy, fire and brilliance, power and incantation of
the verse.

As a final reflection on the needs of this play, the actors would
need an expressive, vigorous and extroverted quality in the physi-

cal playing of most of the characters, many of whom display themselves with great bravura: a sense of realism in action is not enough to convey the dynamics, energy, power and sexuality they possess.

From these two rambles through the director's thinking process (by no means comprehensive) it can be seen that this is the time when good but adventurous judgement must be used, and the priorities of the production and acting determined. Directors use all sorts of means to stimulate their creative ideas, and clarify their decisions: notes, historical research, sketches, models, speaking the text aloud: anything that makes for familiarity with the material and stimulates ideas about the matter, and the means. A play is not a mere mechanical thing to be processed: there are no rules of convention or aesthetics which must be applied to a play of a particular kind to ensure its correct performance. One fundamental consideration only must be borne in mind: what is the nature of the reality, and what are the means best suited to convey it?

3
Staging and the Mise-en-Scène

During recent years we have seen much change in thinking about
theatre buildings, with some of that thinking put into practice.
To many people "theatre" means the conventional playhouse of
the late nineteenth century, itself an adaption of the Italian
opera-house. We must consider the potentialities of the most
commonly found types of theatre building before going on to
think about how to mount plays in them. The conventional
theatre, with multi-level auditorium, fly-tower, and proscenium
arch has certain advantages, namely stage machinery and on
occasions an atmosphere of romance and luxury. Its style of
auditorium and foyer decoration is usually lavish, even if it is
lacking in facilities like adequate bars and lavatories, and implies
that what will be presented on the stage will be romantic and illusory. The facilities of the stage itself presuppose that they should
be used: flown scenery, staging on a revolve, full wall-to-wall
scenery. The building was designed for a particular usage and
seems to define by its very nature what stage scenery should be.
The proscenium is a frame in which to depict near-reality.

" Open " Stages

The open-end stage, that is the acting platform with the audience
in front of it, like a proscenium theatre without a proscenium,
tends to be anti-illusionist, and anti-romantic, since it makes no
attempt to disguise the artifice of scenery and staging. It isn't
anti-scenic or anti-spectacle, however, as it can usually provide a
large acting area, and proportionately more space at the stage
end than a proscenium theatre. It simply calls for scenery of a
different kind, and a stronger emphasis on the use of movement
in a three-dimensional pattern. Lighting, the means of moving
scenery (dress up your stage-hands) and the use of flying equipment and revolves can be seen in operation by the audience, who,
at a generalization, enjoy the experience. Scenery becomes

scenery, not reality, and can be appreciated for more qualities than its capacity to fool us. It can incorporate the structure and space of the building itself, or stand free in the middle of the platform, but it doesn't pretend to be going on beyond the wings. The thrust stage, that is, with an acting platform pushing out into the audience who surround it on three sides, is also anti-illusionist but pro-pictorial, making a close and immediate relationship between actors and audience: obviously it possesses serious limitations in terms of naturalistic settings, and three walls are an impossibility. Many ingenious compromises have been affected at Chichester and other theatres. The National Theatre's production of *Uncle Vanya* made use of an ingenious façade by Sean Kenny: at the back of the stage, the elevation of a house in pine boarding, with reversible windows, and furniture and cupboards built into its surface: this served as both interior and exterior as required, with furniture disposed on the stage in front of it. In the same theatre, a production of *Reunion in Vienna* (a naturalistic play of the 'thirties) was staged in a setting that created two walls of a room, obliquely positioned—a similar setting to that which might be used on an open-end stage.

Theatre in the round shares many of the characteristics of the thrust stage: even greater contact with the audience, intimacy, an acute sense of the physical relationship between characters. However, it presents many more problems to the director in setting and moving the play: only the barest functional necessities can be accommodated, a table and a couple of chairs. Scenic objects in the ordinary sense cannot be used if they obscure the view of the audience above a height of a couple of feet. Finally, there are impromptu acting areas, in which a production can be presented without a stage as such: any space big enough, visible enough for the performance, where the visual emphasis is on the action, grouping and movement of the actors. The growing field of what Peter Brook calls "Rough Theatre" uses plays and entertainments which don't need scenery as such, or make use of improvised scenery, made of sacking and scaffolding, planks and barrels, anything to hand, throwing the play open to the audience's imagination.

Awful Stages

This leaves us with one other type of stage to be considered: the Unsuitable Stage, whether in a hall or a theatre, or devised for all-purpose use and doubling as a concert hall or place of assembly. It characteristics are a high, small stage, no wing-space, no flying-space or load-bearing grid, minimal lighting equipment, and a large, long, narrow, flat auditorium, separated from the stage by a plywood proscenium, bearing the masks of comedy and tragedy! Manifestly such a theatre, in which many talented amateurs have to work, must be modified radically, but not necessarily at great expense, if effective work is to be achieved. Before planning scenery and presentation in these conditions, a summary of the vices of the building must be made. It is possible that the pseudo-theatre is not the most suitable building for mounting a play because the audience's ability to see and hear is of greater importance than the player's convenience.

First, then, can the acting area and the audience be placed in a better relationship? Will the stage accommodate necessary scenery? Has the auditorium a comfortable atmosphere, without excessive distractions of windows, curtains, grand pianos, and so forth? Simple functionality would seem preferable to a gimcrack "theatre" atmosphere. Investment in equipment to improve such a stage is an absolute priority: this may mean temporary staging which must be erected and struck every time the stage is used, but which is still worth the extra effort and staff. It is possible to advance the stage towards the audience by means of an apron or fore-stage or rostra or boards and scaffolding: such an apron could be unified to the stage by means of a stage-cloth. Obviously a large and high fore-stage would be unsuitable in a small building seating up to 150: the more drastic step of lowering the stage itself may be more appropriate, and many such stages are simple structures of joists and boards. An unsuitable proscenium could be removed, unless load-bearing, in which case reveals extending downstage from the proscenium opening could support a false prosc. closer to the audience. A temporary proscenium on an open-ended hall would be suitable for a building in which productions were only mounted occasionally: flats, a header, returns and a soffit, of timber and canvas construction. The Guildhall

School of Music and Drama have been coping resourcefully with a shallow stage and a megalomaniac proscenium for many years, by the simple expedient of incorporating a false proscenium on the forestage into most designs.

Wherever possible, the audience's eyes must be prepared for concentration on the stage itself by painting the proscenium walls a neutral colour, perhaps extending the painting along the first few feet of the auditorium wall, thus giving the impression of a larger stage. Both the Old Vic and the Aldwych theatres have been adapted to large-scale productions by variations of these devices, in the case of the Vic losing the proscenium altogether. Certainly the stage must be made a flexible frame for presentation, and its surrounds must not compete with scenery. Following Lady Bracknell's principles, both stage and auditorium must be changed if necessary. This may mean removing a number of seats, or raking the audience seating to produce adequate sight-lines. The initial expense of portable or collapsible rostra for seating could be recovered with a few more full houses. Lighting must be reviewed: the power supply may need to be increased and the control system may need additional capacity, scaffold barrelling, and long tail lamps. We accept the functional presence of lighting in the open-end theatre, like the Mermaid.

Perhaps the best remedy for the unsuitable stage is to give voice against its building: however, any practical steps that can be taken should take priority over scenery.

Thinking about Scenery

Any increase in the possibilities of staging means that scenic concepts can be revised. The box set, so long a favourite in repertory theatres and the amateur theatre, has been over-used because of its simplicity and suitability to the proscenium theatre. As the repertoires of companies become more adventurous so there is less need to play safe in the field of design. The director need not be a designer, but must be aware of developments in this area: new materials and non-realism.

When thinking about staging a play the reasons for setting must be examined ruthlessly. Scenery and properties cost time, money and effort. There is an apocryphal story of the prop elephant created for Charles Wood's *H*. After vast expense, research, and loving care, the life-sized monster finally made its first appearance at a late rehearsal; as it was trundled on a voice spoke from the stalls: "Cut it." Months later the elephant was on sale to anybody needing such an eccentric article, at a fraction of its original cost. Such comic catastrophes can be averted at the planning stage. The proper considerations are first, what to use out of practical necessity—architecture or natural objects, furniture, things that are used or handled; secondly, whatever is useful to create or enhance atmosphere and reality and create believable environment. Many realistic plays need exactly the right props and furnishing and décor, for example Coward or Wilde would be unthinkable if crudely set. Realistic adornment for its own sake is a temptation to be avoided, as it turns out to be an expense and an encumbrance to action. The purely scenic conditions surrounding the actor are likely to exert a strong influence on the movement and organic action of the play, affecting what the actor does and intimating a mood which he must follow. Sometimes the shape and size of setting is stylized, and has a vital function to play in the develoment of mood and action: for example in the RSC production of *The Government Inspector*, where the perilous world of small-town dignity was set on a very steep rake: movement, and keeping up the character of dignified and pompous citizens, became a precarious business, with a metaphorical banana-skin under every foot.

Without becoming too theoretical, the director needs a good sense of the use of space, and of dimension and proportion. What he puts on stage will condition the blocking he gives to a play, and create a mood: nothing must be used just because a reason can be found, or because it is available or is expected by an audience. As the realistic play has over-exploited the interior box set, so it has nearly established a convention in the use of furnishing: characters hop from one piece of upholstered furniture to another, and are so busy being realistic that nothing physically interesting happens in performances. The relationship of people to objects and things is important and often deeply significant, as both television and film constantly demonstrate. Size, shape, proportion matter: human scale is the first thing we perceive: it is a guide to normal apprehension, so four actors in a realistic thriller moving round an apartment of Piranesian dimensions, in eighteen-foot flats, are having to work against a basic scenic unreality. Proliferation of furniture simply suggests wall-to-wall reality in a huge room, and may be out of keeping with the spirit of the play, unless it's *The New Tenant*. The over-large stage needs reducing to the appropriate size, rather than the scale of the set being increased. Distortion of shapes, colours, and textures has often a strong emotional effect and can establish the characters in a surrealist or terrifying world. Incongruity of setting can determine the mood, as, for example, the model of the Old Bailey in *One Way Pendulum*. This, however, is staging for a deliberate effect, and specified by the dramatist. Scenic possibilities can only be explored by experiment with the materials and space available, and the use of models: such playing around with the proposed setting may bring forth developments as rehearsal develops a play.

I arrived at a setting for *The White Devil*, discussed in the previous chapter, in just such a manner. The play was being staged at RADA's Vanbrugh theatre, a proscenium theatre of fair size, with a large apron. The setting consisted of a circular temple of columns, in the form of two curved screens of huge coloumns, able to revolve round a circular platform, providing both the exterior of a building and, when opened, its interior. The set worked mechanically, looked heavy and severe, and was theoretically ingenious and suitable, but in model form very dull and classical. By accident the model dropped out of alignment: columns reeled and swayed, lintels toppled, and the set leant outward at the top: equilibrium became precarious and collapse imminent. When this earthquake-shaken building was decayed by weather and blackened by fire (suggested by dirty finger marks on the polystyrene model) it suggested the decadent grandeur and madness of Webster's world much more accurately than the original setting.

A shape may determine the pattern of movement during performance. An aborted production of *A Woman of No Importance* used great circular mats on the stage floor, causing the characters to drift idly round in elegant circles, while delivering Wildean witticisms. The floor pattern of movement is very strongly influenced by the position of scenery, and even by the appearance of the stage floor: a set for *Antony and Cleopatra* which I devised round a circular stage cloth, with semicircular rostra, produced endless circling movements, leisurely ambles, and chatty walks: it proved difficult to get any character from *A* to *B* in a direct and unfussy manner. The staging suited Cleopatra, but none of the other characters.

Director/Designer Relationship

Clearly, the relationship between designer and director should begin at the first conception of the production, after both have read the play thoroughly and formed some feelings and impressions, and even perhaps a few concrete ideas. Ideally, there should be an exchange of thoughts, rather than a directive to the designer. It's an awful chore merely to put somebody else's thoughts into a reality and a sympathetic designer with a free hand may provide ideas which capture the essence of the play. This is seldom set down in the text and may trigger off the production: what people wear, how space is used. Michael Annals' vivid, dramatic and delicate costumes and settings for *The Royal Hunt of the Sun* caught the spirit and symbols of the play perfectly: the costumes of the Incas as guardians of the Sun God, the intense emotion generated by Atahuallpa framed in a huge scenic sun of gold. Stimulating ideas are all-important to the director, and the designer can provide them: he is concerned with the play as a series of pictures, each of which should tell part of a story. Direction is a gathering together of many imaginations, emotions, elusive feelings and impressions. Sometimes the design concept must be based on reality, scrupulously re-created: the exact details of a particular time and place, its feel, colour and mood—the social realistic play, for example the Royal Court's fine productions of D. H. Lawrence's miners' trilogy, with sets based on sepia photos, with the roof of a back-to-back house as low as a tall man stooping, rooms and bodies blackened with coal dust; mash from a huge black oven apparently so hot that the character juggled it in his mouth to cool it.

The first consideration at these preliminary discussions is the action, as far as the director can visualize it: how it can help the actor by providing freedom, atmosphere, and reality. The setting which takes attention from the actors within it must be ruthlessly simplified. A recent production by an illustrious designer was spectacular but so difficult to get round that one of the principal actresses had to make her first entrance down a narrow staircase on her bottom; an actor had to deliver a soliloquy from a promontory ten feet above the stage, and his thought as he moved forward was "Which way shall I fall, if I fall off?" Design purely for spectacle is more suitable to the operatic convention, where the use of movement is a mere convenience, a means of changing from one tableau to another. The actor seeks to express himself physically in the fullest way, three-dimensionally; the necessity to cheat into three-quarter profile, to present the face and front to the audience, is inimical to realistic acting.

The director, then, must be deeply involved in the process of design and acquainted with the mechanics of presentation, or he may find that his production is dictated by a setting. All theatrical presentation is false: as one tries to gauge the degree of reality in the acting, so an economical scenic expression must be found which will give the audience and actors a sense of place and mood. It is outside the compass of this book to discuss scenic design in any depth, but it is necessary to summarize a few basic ideas about setting the stage, which the director can put into practice as a design is evolved.

First, realistic and pictorial scenery is secondary to good acting, and can often be dispensed with: where the budget is small, it's unwise to attempt a realistic setting which would be tatty; better to present a simple setting of drapes made into a neat box, with appropriate furniture, to use frame doors and windows, eliminate backings, etc. If a setting is simplified, it must look clean, functional, and stylish. The box set, or the realistic set, needs great ingenuity and good painting: a large set needs variety and long runs of wall made up of flats are dull to look at and liable to wobble. It is advisable to break a, say, fifteen-foot run of flat with a one-foot return. Disproportionate height and size should be avoided: a play which clearly demands a small interior should have a reasonable-sized set, which may mean that the set is either placed within the stage, surrounded by neutral drapes, or that the proscenium is narrowed by tormentors on either side and a border above. This means that the idea of a realistic "fourth wall" must be abandoned: Jimmy Porter's attic flat cannot be thirty-two feet wide! Alternatively, the setting on a tiny stage must reveal behind the proscenium part of a room or interior to the right scale and not try to scale an embassy down to an area fourteen feet by ten. Allowance must be made when laying out a setting for areas which are outside the set proper: hallways, other rooms, gardens, etc. A painted cloth one foot from a window cannot be satisfactorily lit, and actors must be able to make easy exits and entrances, with room for standby prop tables in off-stage areas. Space must also be allowed for adequate bracing of the box set: a farce with five doors constantly being opened and shut needs a very strong and rigid structure.

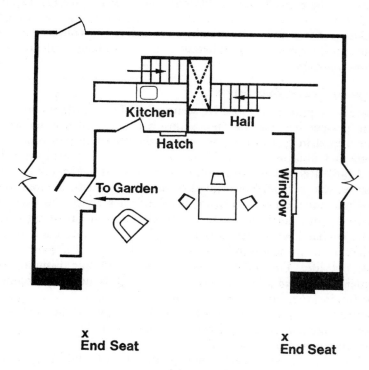

Fɪɢ 1   *Ground plan of stage*

Allowance must also be made for removal and changing of scenery and props, and for space in which to act! So much must be crammed into the small space of the stage that a preliminary ground plan must be made before the design is finalized. This must be to scale, and drawn on a scale plan of the stage itself.

The box setting on page 39 is a preliminary layout for *The Birthday Party* and shows the basic necessities of the set: space for action, relative to the main furniture, sight-lines and access to the set; and the position of entrances and windows. It can be seen that something on these lines could proceed, since the set fulfils certain basic requirements. These are: (1) space to move the actors with freedom; (2) reasonable wing-space, with room for lighting back-ings, windows, etc.; (3) a window placed to provide a natural light source, which needs little masking: the actor can stand upstage of it to look out; (4) entrances that present the actor: Meg's entrance down the stairs can be seen before she comes into the room; (5) reasonable architectural logic, making a degree of realism possible.

Types of Scenic Experience

The use of painted perspective scenery, or of structures incorpora-ting perspectives, has become almost a convention in itself. It is much used in pantomine and opera, where a quality of romanti-cism and illusion is needed: the basic materials are again flats and built scenery, with the addition of painted cloths, cut cloths, gauzes, and brilliantly executed *trompe-l'œil* effects. Though the original intention was realism, this kind of scenery has become a very subtle medium, since it uses the convention of pictorial art. Art has been widely popularized, and if we are consciously referring to its ways and means we tend to be commenting on art, not life. The webby, romantic set, a Gothic Elsinore, of *Rosencrantz and Guildenstern are Dead*, was not just another set for *Hamlet*, but a mad world in which a lurid and incompre-hensible melodrama was being played out, not by the down-to-earth Rosencrantz and Guildenstern but by the illusory world in which they had no proper role.

The thrust stage has become modified with the attempts to make it serve all the ends of modern theatre. The architecture of the Elizabethan theatre clearly will not suit a wide variety of plays, and the gain in intimacy and immediacy in relationship with the audience is offset by the inconvenience and compromise necessary. Trying to draw some idea of what sort of a stage we now have, it seems that the floor has become a significant piece of scenery, together with the vertical elevation behind the actors, that is, the back wall. Various treatments are possible: the atmosphere of *The Birthday Party* by horrible lino, fading rugs, and the architecture and wallpaper of only one wall; equally *The White Devil* by magnificent Roman floors of marble and one titanic wall. Heavy boards, sand, leaves and artificial grass are other possibilities. Certainly realism is limited to things which can be seen and appreciated for their values of colour, texture and surface, rather than for disposition of mass of for architectural qualities, and the imagination of the designer in discovering the scenic metaphor is all-important. Returning to *The Royal Hunt of the Sun*, Annals used a huge metallic shield, emblazoned with the cross of the Conquistadores, which opened out like an unfolding flower to become the Sun of the Inca God-King.

Theatre in the round throws the emphasis on the actor entirely: not only scenery, but even composition of grouping, is subordinate to human figures and movement. The only scenic possibilities are the stage floor and anything hung above the actor's heads, a sort of scenic sandwich. Obviously the eye of the audience must not be continually directed upwards, nor must anything flown impede the lighting; however, the atmosphere of *Hamlet* can be created by the structural ribs of a Gothic roof, and *The Long and the Short and the Tall* by a broken and sagging roof of bamboo and palm leaves. The emphasis, however, must remain on the realism and workability of costumes and props: accuracy of make-up, and above all truthful acting: even the glamorous heroine's scent must be in character!

Scenery cannot make a production: it is like the sauce to a dish, adding flavour, heightening the enjoyment. Just as a bad sauce can overwhelm the flavour, so the wrong scenery can distract us from the play and its characters, or spoil it altogether. As the most expensive single item in the mounting of a play, economy must be our first consideration: the actors may change their performances, the play may become more entertaining or more enlightening as rehearsals proceed: but a set, once put into solid reality, is the most inflexible and unchangeable thing about the whole production, and may make or mar it.

New Acting Spaces

Some years ago, Michael Elliott gave an important broadcast in which he deplored the innundation of theatre by monumental buildings and civic pomp, which buildings, of course, impose the need for lavish and expensive productions. Happily, since then there has been a creative avalanche of "rough" theatre in diverse forms; fringe plays, touring productions aimed at potential audiences without a theatre building, Theatre in Education, entertainments, satires, and cabarets, street theatre, one and two-man shows, etc. This movement has proved a tremendous liberation from the tyranny of expensive buildings and the exorbitantly priced scenery required to fill their stages. It means, at the very least, theatre where there was none before, and a revaluing of the nature and quality of scenic spectacle. Design values must be superb to justify the enormous cost of this.

Simple theatre, however, must have its own aesthetic, which is internal and organic, and needs no less thought and effort. Rough Theatre doesn't mean tatty theatre. *Space* is the main requirement, and all too often there is a pretence that a room over a pub, a small hall, is a "real" theatre, that is, an old-fashioned one-directional theatre. Actors and their movement, grouping and choreography, costumes, make-up, properties, furnishings and weapons must withstand close scrutiny and must be visually stunning and utterly right. An impromptu acting area is a well chosen place, indoors or outdoors; it may be a pavement with a banana skin dropped on a pavement, an actor on a one-wheel bicycle, or a dress over the back of a chair in an empty room. And actors. Audience positions must be craftily manipulated so that the maximum number can see and hear without background distractions or noise, movement, or lights. A certain formality of seating arrangements makes an improvised theatre into a ceremonial, ritual place, and makes any acting area important and exciting, whether the effect is intended to be that of a round, a square, a promenade or a thrust "stage". Actors and a play will fare better on a flat space against a plain wall than on a tiny "unsuitable" stage, as even a small stage pre-supposes some degree of scenic spectacle, which is nearly impossible to provide. The director and actors must develop a good hunch for "locations" as sometimes there's only ten minutes to decide *where* the magic tryst occurs.

Gorgeous and practical new theatres have been built (and some expensive monsters) and old theatres glamorously restored: they cry out for the uttermost artistry, effort, and expense in design (see Manchester Royal Exchange and Glasgow Citizen's Theatre, who provide all these). There will always be an audience for the visual delight, compelling watchability which the conventional well-equipped theatre can provide but these qualities must also exist in "rough" theatre—it's a matter of standards, not scale.

4
The Actor and Acting

Knowledge of the actor and his art is the most powerful skill the director can possess, and without it he is nothing. Actors are so diverse in their talents and personalities that it is very difficult to state absolutes about the art of the performer. The progress of an acting career may change utterly over a period of years, and Romeo may turn into a character comedy actor and the character comédienne from the variety stage reveal a talent for serious roles. The directors an actor encounters over the years can contribute much to his continued training, and by their influence and guidance open doors to new roles and new skills; equally, a bad director may prevent an actor from developing, discourage him and throttle his talent. The responsibility for continuing the actor's growth is one of the pleasures of directing, and there will be many occasions in a lifetime of directing when the director must teach the actor, for the truly talented and receptive actor is always eager to learn.

Often gifted and celebrated actors pronounce against any sort of training except experience: they have succeeded without going to a school of drama or taking acting lessons, and genuinely believe that a logical basis for acting skill is destructive to the spontaneous nature of the work. Such actors probably have more than the average share of physical endowments, plus intuition and high imagination, and by working for many years with talented and craftsmanlike actors and actresses they have in fact received many hundreds of acting lessons. The passing on of the art of acting will always fall to the fine performer, since other actors will try to emulate him; but with the rise of the director, that role is now shared, and even an actor of great talent would be prepared to learn something from Peter Brook, a Jonathan Miller or John Dexter. The pressure of rehearsal is so intense that very often it is spent simply organizing, and packaging a product: this means that often the actor, with his skills and qualities, is taken for granted, and there is little time for experiment and developing the actor beyond the requirements of his or her role. In the process of a few weeks rehearsal, an actor can achieve much more than the know-how necessary for the part: every role offers the chance to polish and improve his technique. The actor generally welcomes an interest in his actual means of performance, and enjoys the process of being "stretched," which is not being asked to do the impossible but being asked to reach to the limit of his capacity, to project the voice more, to play high comedy with delicacy and lightness, to move with more agility or more control. Stanislavsky was the first great artist of the theatre to rationalize the creative process (though not its end product), and the consideration of the actor's means is one way the director can help him toward a performance.

The Actor as Himself: The Actor as Mimic

There has always been argument as to whether acting is a creative or interpretative art. Alec Guinness describes the actor as a craftsman, having, and using, skill, technique, and method as a musician, dancer, or painter does. Certainly the good actor exercises craftsmanship, but there is an extra dimension. The actor cannot be equated with the instrumental musician, who reads a score and, under the guidance of the conductor, makes music. The musical instrument and the human instrument cannot be compared, except on the vocal level: the human being possesses many capacities for conveying experience, ideas, and feeling. In most good acting, both creativeness and interpretation must be apparent. Acting cannot be dictated: its tempo and volume can be adjusted, but its effect is not emotive and abstract like music but precise and unique: there is no way of scoring human behaviour. At some stage, characters come to believable life. Intention, clarity, meaning and motives, repose and economy: all these are constituents of a good performance, but do not alone, when allied to the playwright's text, make the actor credible as the character he's playing. The nature of acting would seem to be, first, the ability to tell a story, then to add to it by living a human experience. The actor as story-teller and sufferer seems to fall somewhere between two extremes, which

the French define as *Acteur* and *Comédien*. The first category
is for the actor who expresses joy and suffering through his own
personality, his own voice, movement, habits of expression:
always himself, recognizable yet presenting ideas with sensitivity,
feeling, humour, coherence. He or she immediately engages our
interest, as representative of ourselves, less inhibited, more articulate. Gielgud has always appeared thus, able to realize a character
through his own outward expression, without losing any of its
human, intellectual or psychological possibilities. Nor is it only
the great tragic actor (though Gielgud is a fine comedy player)
who acts mainly through the medium of his own personality.
Comic actors, from Chaplin to Richard Briers, mainly present
one personality, a man more vulnerable yet more resilient than
ourselves, whose experiences are often close to tragic. Even the
film star, the glamorous and frivolous personality, must not be
underestimated: though every performance may seem the
same, they are always credible, and those characteristics of
chic, nonchalance, elegance or even ordinariness are often the
product of years of practice and polish.

At the other end of the acting scale is the impersonator, seldom
himself. Adept at disguise, a brilliant mimic, fascinated by the
externals of people's appearance, speech, motion, he sets about
acting by assuming another personality. He may lose much of
himself in the process, though many great impersonating actors
have characteristics which cannot be disguised: Olivier, for example, with a voice of brass and an articulation of great muscularity. However, Olivier does demonstrate most fully the practice
of the *Comédien*, with carefully conceived make-up, imaginative
use of movement and exploration of the range and possibilities
of the voice. Compare his performance as Othello, Astrov, and
the Captain in *The Dance of Death*.

To what extent the actor performs as himself, or assumes an
impersonation, is dependent on his own personality, his reasons
for acting. Every role uses to some degree the actor's own
psychology, and certain acting media, like film and television,
demand a scrupulously truthful and lifelike quality of acting,
where impersonation would appear false and theatrical: in such
media, the actor is cast very much as himself. It is very hard to
make a judgement on an actor's abilities without having seen

a variety of performances, and a director must try to gauge, from previous work, how the actor's ability and temperament operate. The ability to judge the performers' potential also depends on being able to draw a distinction between what is intuitive and what has been learned from experience. Some actors are very gifted in terms of good expressive speech and movement, without being imaginative; others are lacking in skill, but possess great power in communicating feeling and emotion. The untrained actor may possess judgement, understanding and sensibility, but lack the power to project and to sustain a performance: the commonest acting fallacy is that deeply felt emotion will touch and excite an audience, and the experienced actor learns to substitute technique for inspiration.

We should consider those general accomplishments required of the actor, whatever the effect of his personality or whatever parts he plays, together with the means of achieving them. Imagination, emotional expressiveness, the abilty to learn, develop and modify a role are the basic mental qualities, the use of voice and speech and relaxed but dynamic use of the body the physical. Clive Swift, himself a director and teacher as well as an actor, recently said that one quality he looked for in the actor was energy. Energy, like vocal intensity, is power: controlled or realized, suffusing or lacking, the speed, strength, and weight of action, movement, and speech. It is not simply effort or tension, but rather a degree of vitality or vibrancy which exists even in repose. Consider the brooding Cleopatra:

> Give me to drink Mandragora. . . .

or Lear:

> Thou'lt come no more,
> Never, never, never, never, never.
> . . . . Pray you undo this button.

A characterization may be founded on the energy implicit in the role, its possession, fruitful or destructive use, waste, or loss. The frightening thing about Lear is that he's over eighty years old, and has an unnatural superabundance of it. He must suffer

dreadful journeyings, neglect, starvation, the brutality of the
elements, insult, nakedness, shock, madness, confusion, rage,
hate, and the death of those he loves before the terrible fire of
energy is at last extinguished.

An interesting parallel in the importance of energy can be
drawn between Lear and Jarry's awful King Ubu, monarch of
the graffiti board: foaming invectives and obscenities, in a
perpetual convulsion of mirth, terror, suspicion, greed, vanity,
and violence, he too is conspicuous for his awe-inspiring vigour,
and like Lear passes through all that a cruel and meaningless
fate can hurl at him. The difference is that Pa Ubu is a hugely
comic survivor, and hurls it right back.

Cleopatra has the energy of a great snake: coiling, curving,
twining, making beautiful and fantastic Arabesques, changing
and glittering; then suddenly striking, shrieking with bared
fangs, throwing her powerful coils round her victim. She is a
great and profound voluptuary, and differs from us in the
intensity and richness of her sensations. We should breathe,
feel, vibrate and shudder with her.

Every dramatist's character worth playing exists in terms of
energy, the surge and ebb of vitality. This elusive ingredient is
what powers good acting, acting with feeling, and helps the
actor to sustain a communication with the audience: to lift
them into laughter, to make them listen. Energy can only come
from a most economical use of all the actor's resources.

The Training of the Actor

There is much controversy about the training and rehearsal of
the actor. Training falls into three general areas: the training
of the mind and imagination, the voice and speech, and movement. The means of preparing the actor's mind is by improvisation, whether it takes the form of exercises or of rehearsal: what
is rehearsal but improvising, experimenting, for finding the best
means of expressing the vaguest or profoundest imaginings, and
for discovering the minutiae of behaviour. All too often it is used
as a time for polishing superficial judgements into acceptable
dramatic expression. Improvisation is a much abused exercise,
often becoming an end in itself, but it remains the basic exercise

in acting. Its object would seem to be to enable the actor to explore his imagination, to induce a process whereby one idea leads to another: to enrich and deepen spontaneous thought. The actor's conscious, intellectual judgement of people and situations is usually readily accessible and what is sought taneous, which is stored in the subconscious. The actor must have freedom from his own inhibitions, prejudices and judgements, and his sophistication both as an actor and a person: for example, to project oneself back into one's youth is difficult: mature comment on youthful idiocies, and naïveté will creep in, even in the form of humour: the actor may present a comment on youth, rather than youth itself. The actor is perilously insecure, and knows that he must undergo an emotional breast-baring before an audience: what more natural than that he should resort to a defensive posture of externalized comment, and present a clever and facile demonstration of the role, rather than be the role, the only criterion as far as the audience are concerned? Many distinguished actors have during recent years shown their distaste for improvisatory exercises, deeming them to be a waste of time (often quite rightly). This is fair enough: the actor who can claim to have moved or amused audiences for thirty years has not only the ways and means but access to a profound imagination, acquired through thousands of hours of rehearsal. The very experienced actor inevitably moves toward roles which suit him and in which he can best serve the public, the dramatist, and his fellow actors.

If we allow that some actors prefer the improvisation of rehearsal to the exercise in general, we must allow that it is infinitely beneficial to the young actor and the actor in training. The mature or trained actor has little opportunity or encouragement to continue his development and training. All he can usually do is draw commonsense conclusions from his experience, and hope to put them into practice. No other performing artist does so little to increase his skill and keep it up to scratch: the actor should be encouraged to emulate musicians, singers, and dancers, with frequent voice and movement workouts, and acting workshops. The RSC and the National Theatre run their own workshops to offer their actors further training and access to specialist skills, and the ordinary working actor, amateur or professional, must use whatever training is available to him. We must have clear objectives in mind: to discover something about the actor, or the play. It must be used with economy: an improvisation to explore an aspect of human psychology is used to arrive at a better understanding of human phenomena; at some stage, it must be transmuted into acting. Two comedians improvising a routine with custard pies or buckets of whitewash may need to improvise for many days, and even the final product may be improvisatory when performed since it depends entirely on the laughter of the audience. The director must be the observer of all that is spontaneously discovered or revealed, and must help the actor to use any results. The actor obviously requires to improvise in rehearsal only when a creative result is not forthcoming: to explore a character, or situation in depth, to solve the problem of either understanding or expressing it. Improvisation used as an exercise not only helps the actor toward creativeness, by getting the mental juices flowing, but reveals him to himself: self-knowledge is an obvious necessity for the actor, but he must acquire it rather than have it thrust upon him. The actor's effect on his fellow actors is the starting point for his effect on the audience, his *raison d'être*. In the freedom of the rehearsal room he can discover his emotional resources, limitations and assets of expressiveness without feeling that he is in any way failing the collective effort of a performance. A group of intelligent actors can usually provide a rationalization for anything with dramatic possibilities, but this is not acting: the ideas are separated from the means of conveying them. When a motivation has been established, the actor must live out the situation or the character, identify with it, believe in it. Thus he escapes from his personal isolation, and the worries of the actor's deadlines, words and moves. This is the inspirational part of acting, which finally must turn into technique: the moving spirit cannot be expected to last to the two-hundredth performance! The actor observes, stores up human experience, and often forgets or suppresses it. This is the ore to be mined during improvisation.

The Use of Improvisation: The Actor's Emotions and Creativity

Let us consider an improvisation exercise, and what might

emerge from it. The object was to explore a subject that might be alarming to many actors, and which is attended by many popular misconceptions and even jokes: lunacy, and various kinds of mental disorder, of which, as of death, injury, blindness and a host of other disasters the actor can have little experience! The play in rehearsal was the curious *Marat/Sade* by Peter Weiss, fascinating for its use of theatrical ways and means. This is a play of considerable complexity, where within the play another play is enacted, the murder of the revolutionary Jean-Paul Marat by Charlotte Corday. The play within the play is enacted by the inmates of an asylum for the insane or anti-social (wherein De Sade was for a long time incarcerated) and purports to be written and directed by the Marquis himself. It is a vehicle for a debate on the nature and attainment of freedom between Marat and De Sade, reflections on revolution by the ascetic on the one hand and the self-gratifying sensualist on the other. It presents a series of tableaux of the horrific consequences of revolution, the sufferings of the oppressed, and uses the means of total theatre—acting, songs, mime, spectacle, narrative—and embraces every mood from tragedy to pantomime comedy. The principal alienation device of the play is to make many of its most important statements be uttered by lunatic characters, so that what they say is divorced from convincing and realistic motivation, and may be considered as fact, not opinion. Marat, for example, is acted by a patient suffering from paranoia; most of the other patients are victims of psychological disorders, emotional upheaval, mental deficiency, or disease which has mental consequences. Weiss has specified that variously they are suffering from depression, erotomania, mania, and in the case of the patient playing Corday, sleeping sickness. Some are merely violently antisocial or nonconformist, as in the case of the four singers, who are down-and-out alcoholics. Most of the patients have no name, and no individuality but their madness. Before these conditions could be acted, they had to be simply comprehended, and the actors undertook some research into cause and effect. So intense, moving, and important a human condition as madness deserves realistic acting. It is at this stage of investigating human behaviour that the actor and director can get bogged down in a mass of imperfectly understood or superfluous psychological data, and it must be clearly appreciated that motive and behaviour which communicates itself to the audience are what is being sought. Enough to be believable and economical: one of the most criticized aspects of "Method" acting has been the lack of economy, the adornment of the role with justifiable but irrelevant actions and implications.

The subject was worked on collectively at first, the actors improvising their chosen condition: trying to express it, feel it, and establish relationship, or the lack of it, with each other. For a long period the result was a group of dull, withdrawn, aggressive characters, very similar to each other: the actors were naturally reticent about using their own fears, phobias, and capacity for violence. The likely reality, that mental disorder diminishes and maims expression, had to be reconsidered, because it revealed too little for the purpose of theatre. The representation of madness and idiocy was then explored in a very theatrical way, treating it as a romantic subject, exaggerating behaviour and attitudes. This more superficial treatment in this case produced a more useful result, as the actors were in better control of their actions: a useful conclusion might be that thought without coherent expression doesn't work theatrically, and that some reality is far from theatrical reality. Purely physical things conveyed themselves, though emerging from the thoughts of the actors: the herald giggling inanely in the middle of a solemn speech, Corday mincing a bouquet of flowers between her fingers, faces aghast with effort, a huge man stumping about on uncontrolled legs. Out of a great quantity of material produced, each actor was able to develop something: one actor produced a quiet, simple fellow who prayed with desperate earnestness, another an idiotically grinning man who occasionally broke into misery, and cursed and muttered under his breath. Gradually a varied group of "patients" came to life, all of whom were articulate enough to deliver lines and sing songs, and capable of movement, whatever bodily disabilities they were portraying.

This is merely the description of improvisation used for a particular purpose, not a description of how to use it. There is no scientific method which guarantees results, and the director's only aim should be to stimulate the actor's imagination, in the hope that something truthful and expressive will emerge. The problem of the group improvisation is that the actor tends for some time to play safe, to imitate the other actor, rather than react to him: so occasionally the objectives must be changed, or an actor asked to do something specific which will induce greater reaction. The actor's use of emotion can sometimes be helped by improvisation, though seldom in the case of mature actors whose personality is very stable since he or she will probably be well aware of the strength and weakness of their emotions: it is tempting to want to help the actor to another string to his bow, but should be resisted. When a less experienced actor develops a "block," and cannot or will not feel or express an emotion, the reason must be sought. The problem may be in the text so that the actor finds the lines false, imprecise, or "not him"; there may be a lack of motivation, or build-up; or the difficulty may be purely personal to the actor: nervousness, or inhibition. A simplification, a concentration on the essential feeling, may produce a result. The only object of the parallel improvisation, that is, taking a simpler situation, with few words, and trying to generate the same feelings, is to free the actor, to take away part of the problem, and make it easier for him to reach a particular objective. The director, in talking to the actor, must find out, if possible, what stimulates emotion and feeling, and ask him to improvise using these particular stimuli: it may be that the actor simply can't get warmed up over the dramatic situation: to analogize simply, Juliet may get more real emotion out of thinking of the death of her cat than out of the death of Romeo. The actor trying to discover and express extreme or subtle emotions is highly sensitive and defensive. The director must give him uncritical support, interest, and understanding.

When an improvisation becomes embarrassing to the actor to the point of inhibiting him, it must be broken off. Annoying him is slightly different: an actor with his dander up may produce what is required. Actors must never be criticized for the quality of text that they can invent off the cuff: many dull actors can create reams of banal dialogue, many good ones can't say a word. The object is not extempore verbalizing, and improvised acting has no effective theatrical quality. We tend to think we know how people behave, what makes them tick: the facile improvisation is a lightning sketch, a caricature of superficially observed characteristics, and when this happens we must break off, and try to probe deeper, to look for other aspects of character which may contribute something contrasting. The actor must be invited to question all aspects of the role, of the character's life. For example, the actor exploring the role of the soldier can resort to an obvious stereotype: a posh voice for an officer, gorblimey for the corporal, plus a set of stock mannerisms, on the assumption that all soldiers are very conventional people (like stage vicars). To improvise is to pay more than lip service to the other possibilities inherent in the character. Does he fear wounding or death? Improvise his death on the battlefield. Why did he become a soldier? Go back to the day he enlisted. What sort of a man is he off duty? Make him talk to his wife. What does he think of his duty to country, other people, himself? The contemporary colonel is a far cry from Lord Cardigan. Improvise a soldier performing the ceremonials, to find out what is impressive, powerful and ridiculous about such trivial acts as drill. The building of a characterization is hard to describe: the effect of characterization is motivation, individuality, life—the character cannot be merely externally applied, it must arise from intuition and experience. When a session of improvisation is fruitful, the director is presented with many new ideas and possibilities, and must remember what has been produced, even if he has to take notes. (A director needs a fathomless memory.) He must also have the courage to persist, to take time, extra time if necessary. An actor in creative difficulties must be helped till he's over them.

The Actor's Concentration

A further important offshoot of improvisation as a training method is the acquisition of concentration, mental tidiness, the ability to think selectively, in a narrow area. To most actors concentration is difficult without physical tension: the product of the actor's thought is evanescent, or he is tossed about by his emotions, and thinks with his heart and his guts. The actor is very susceptible, sensible to stimuli long before he can recognize what it is. A tense actor is looking for what he cannot find, since by his tension he is blocking emotion, clear thinking, and spontaneous inventiveness. The first step to proper concentration is the practice of relaxing physically, of cultivating a sense of physical well-being. The vocal and bodily instrument can only work effectively if prepared. Probably the most common fear of the actor is drying, or losing the thread of continuity—a very basic worry. Few actors worry about the quality or nature of their interpretation or characterization if they have been adequately rehearsed, but they do worry about making the most elementary sorts of fools of themselves. Stage fright, that is the loss of one's self-possession, has all sorts of familiar and unpleasant side effects: constricted speech, breath out of control, wooden or quaking limbs—enough to ruin the start of a performance, or make rehearsal a slow process. Here the actor is preparing to meet a problem by fighting it or running away. The good actor works harder, with less effort because he has evolved a method of combating physical and mental strain; not because he has ceased to be in a blue funk. Nerves are necessary: excitement, awe, fear, a sense of challenge, are essential to a good performance; it's like a combat, which must be won. To lose the combat is to lose the audience's sympathy, to bore them.

Physical Relaxation

To improvise, and to rehearse properly, teaches the actor that he can draw on more than conscious knowledge: he learns to think calmly, not to rush to quick conclusions; to relax mentally, sure that he is in contact with creativeness. Panic is the enemy, and finds physical expression: a worried actor looks worried. Before rehearsal and especially before performance, the actor should prepare himself with a simple process of physical exercise, however briefly it is carried out. Six deep breaths in the wings help control the diaphragm, but aren't quite enough. I suggest the following sequence.

The Face. We tend to wear a mask of habit on it. It needs to be flexible and responsive. Stretch and purse the lips, screw up the eyes and open wide, frown and release the frown, inflate the cheeks. Waggle the jaw from side to side, open wide, bite, and waggle again. Grimace freely, wriggle the scalp until there is some movement. The mask must feel loose but elastic, jaw and mouth free.

The Head. Roll it gently clockwise and anti-clockwise several times, letting it come to rest thrown forward and thrown back. All rolling movement of the head to be done without force, or movement of the shoulders: it's the neck and the pharynx that must be relaxed: head mobility is particularly important to listening.

The Shoulders. Roll and stretch them forward and back, at least a dozen times; raise and let them drop the same number of times. Stretch up with the arms, and let them drop; swing the arms freely and shake the hands till they feel loose and relaxed. Shoulder tension and fluttery or wooden hands are obvious signs of tension, and can happen even to good actors!

The Torso. Quickly pull the solar plexus in and out, breathe deeply several times. A quavering voice is due to a fluttering diaphragm, so expel several breaths from the diaphragm. Rotate the whole torso from the hips, swinging the arms freely round the body, gradually letting head and shoulders droop until the torso is bent over and the spine fully relaxed.

Legs. Shake and swing each leg. Do a little bump and grind with the hips. Bounce on the ball of the foot. Transfer the body weight from foot to foot, with the feet in various positions, forwards and backwards, from side to side: feel your body in balance through the balls of the feet. Check that posture is upright and easy, the back not hollowed, and the head neither thrust forward (common to poor-sighted actors) nor held too far back. The actor's preparatory exercises are as important as the singer's or the athlete's: they improve movement, speech, and concentration, and help to overcome self-consciousness. No actor can afford to spend several minutes pulling himself together in public view!

Learning a Text

If the actor's main anxiety is the fear of drying, or forgetting, anything that can help the learning process will eliminate a host of other worries. Every actor has his own method and speed in the matter of study, and circumstances and habit will contribute to his efficiency. A busy stage actor, or an actor making weekly appearances in a television series will be practised in digesting a text fairly rapidly. Quite simply, age, that is middle age and onward, and infrequency of study, make it harder. The actor who has a study problem must start learning as soon as possible: nobody can be spontaneous when fishing for words: perilous, but not spontaneous! Distinguished actors, used to the slower tempo of films and long runs, often feature in the notices as being unsure of their words, which does them and the paying public less than justice. Again, the benefit of improvisation can be felt in the actor with easy access to the subconscious, where the words should be stored. It is a popular myth that when the practised improviser dries he will make up ad-lib dialogue nearly as good as the text: he won't, but he'll paraphrase fairly capably, and get back on the rails fairly soon. Learning lines is always hard, but is one of those basic things like getting to work. The process can be helped by knowing in some detail the content of the role, and the play itself. This may necessitate paraphrasing the actions, thoughts, intentions, and words, and writing them down. The actor should know the content of every scene, what happens in terms of ideas, and also the "feel" of the scene, what is happening emotionally, and how it changes. This is the bone structure of study, and is grossly neglected in the amateur theatre, and by the overworked actor. Parrot-fashion study, passing a postcard down the page, is less taxing and more mechanical, but involves learning in an exact sequence: the actor given a wrong cue may be completely thrown. The tape-recorder is a useful means of checking on textual accuracy, as well as on verbal clarity and the overall shape of delivery.

I have dwelt this long on the actor's learning process because creativeness can't happen when study is a problem. More good performances have been stifled because the priority for the actor has been knowing the part than from any other cause. It's the actor's first responsibility and finally he is answerable for his own performance.

The Actor's Thoughts about the Role

We must consider the way in which a constructive actor thinks about playing a part. Every actor of any experience consciously or unconsciously takes apart the role "on paper" before reassembling it as a living person. Assuming that the part is worth playing, the actor's first question must be "Why me?" He or she will then start to read through the play, and the first answer to the question may well be because the part is like the actor, in the broadest general terms of personality. Another answer might be that the role needs certain technical skills that the actor possesses: a quality of voice, speech, or movement; or even that the actor's previous experience is useful to the playing of the part, though the resemblance seems to end there. At various times in the last few years, the actor, in an attempt to reconcile himself to the character he's playing, has been encouraged to speculate at great length about the circumstances of the character, by writing hypothetical pasts, presents, and futures. This seems often irrelevant, since so much can be inferred from the text itself, and whilst the actor certainly must be sensitively aware of what might have shaped the character, and have a general understanding of the influences and circumstances that have led that person to that point in his or her fictitious history, too much importance must not be attached to purely hypothetical events.

The next two questions the actor might ask are, first, what does the character look like? How does the character speak? From these two points a chain of inquiry starts. What is the period of the play? Of what nationality are the characters? Of what social class? Does the quality of period, nationality and class matter, or are the characters human types undergoing typical human experiences? These qualities are profoundly important in social comedy, or the comedy of manners, but it is not dramatically useful to think of Sir Toby Belch most specifically as an Illyrian (Yugoslavian): it is necessary to think of Trofimov as a Russian. What does the character say, directly, or by inference, about himself, and what do all the other characters say about him? The dichotomy may be a central point in his character, as for example, Captain Parolles, a boaster, liar, and coward:

PAROLLES. Noble heroes, my sword and yours are kin. Good sparks
and lustrous, a word, good metals: you shall find in the
regiment of the Spinnii one Captain Spurio, with his
cicatrice, an emblem of war, here on his sinister cheek;
it was this very sword entrenched it. Say to him I
live. . . .

The inference is that Parolles, for all his monstrous faults, his deplorable character, is human, LIKEABLE, indeed even sensible. The clever and severely judging Helena thinks so. This is the key to the character, and is paramount above all his other qualities: we can't help warming to him.

HELENA.   . . . I love him for his sake;
And yet I know him a notorious liar,
Think him a great way fool, solely a coward;
Yet these fix'd evils so fit in him
That they take place when virtue's steely bones
Looks bleak i' th' cold wind. . . .

What are the intentions of the character, and his relations with others, and what is his effect on people, both conscious and unconscious? Consider Koolyghin, from *The Three Sisters*: a good man; idealistic, pedantic, a schoolmaster; unconsciously comic and irritating to Masha because he WILL lecture people, and is easily diverted to petty aims ("I've actually been awarded the Order of St Stanislav . . . Second Class").

Today is Sunday, my friends, a day of rest; let us rest and enjoy it, each according to his age and position in life! We shall have to roll up the carpets and put them away till winter. . . . We must remember to put some Napthaline on them, or Persian Powder. . . . The Romans enjoyed good health because they knew how to work AND how to rest. They had *mens sana in corpore sano*. Their life had a definite shape, a form. . . . The director of the school says that the most important thing about life is form. . . . A thing that loses its form is finished—that's just as true of our ordinary, everyday lives. (*Takes Masha round the waist and laughs.*) Masha loves me. Yes, and the curtains will have to be put away with the carpets, too. . . . I'm cheerful today, I'm in quite excellent spirits. . . .

There is a wealth of information here about the character's relationships and intentions. Koolyghin lives a self-sacrificing life, according to the highest principles: he feels deeply, but simply: the intellectual part of his life and the emotional part are not fused together: he just doesn't realize that he's a worthy bore and a bit of an ass. All that knowledge, all that opinion, and where does it get him? Cuckoldom and humiliation.

The actor must try to divine the way the character feels, the way he undergoes emotion, what amuses him, bores him, interests or distresses him. Emotion, intention, and effect are deeply inter-twined and this leads the actor to the reflection: how instru-mental is this character in the events that happen; how much a mere observer or commentator, how much affected by outward, circumstantial things? This of course is merely a brief summary of the first reflections of the actor, but they are the foundation stones of the final performance. As with the director, the actor's creative process starts with his first reading of the play. He will observe certain priorities, and must be sure that they are the right ones.

The Actor's Skills

We must now consider the training and accomplishments of the actor. The director should aim to help the actor as a technician: the actor who does not acquire a solid skill, who depends on inspiration at every performance, will remain a dilettante, how-ever gifted. The foremost of the actor's skills is the use of voice and speech: most of his effective communication is vocal, and a poor voice and badly managed speech will suffice to make him a mediocre actor. We must define voice and speech before pro-ceeding. Voice is the basic instrument: it has musicality, timbre, intonation and size. Speech is the capacity to use words, and endow them with meaning and clarity. To understand their effect on the listening audience, we must think that in broad terms, voice conveys the emotions and physical state of the speaker: speech expresses his ideas and thinking process.   An actor capacity for utterance must learn to make the best of the instru ment: to extend it to the limit of its possibilities.

Breathing and Voice

The young actor is fascinated by problems of interpretation, character and emotion, ideas and presentation, and is not always aware of the basic vocal needs, which should be as exacting as those of the singer. First is audibility: this requires breath and clarity of articulation. It is a commonplace assumption that middle-class English speech is an adequate medium for acting: in fact its breathing is usually shallow, and articulation cramped and affected. (Consider a Kensington version of "The cat sat on the mat," with the vowels slightly distorted to convey an emphatic idea of social class thus: "The cet set on the met.") Such a striking distortion of a vowel sound, with the other vowels similarly mangled is a characterization of affectation in itself. The actor must make use of as much of the thorax as possible by practising rib-reserve breathing, that is releasing the diaphragm when breathing in as well as expanding the rib cage, thereby increasing the breath capacity. On giving voice he has a flexible means of expelling breath, the diaphragm, making for quick and powerful attack, and a steady means: the deflation of the rib cage. Breath held in reserve in the rib cage gives the actor voice to spare, hence flexibility in speaking long passages that do not permit of pausing. Running out of breath is a common cause of inaudibility: volume fades away at the end of the line or sentence. The untrained actor must learn to use the punctuation of the text as a blueprint for breathing: a snatched breath for a comma, a full breath on a stop, colon or semicolon. Thus he will learn to take in breath at different speeds, and also to give the text a rough shape as the writer intends. Breathing is the foundation of the actor's energy, vibrancy and control of the voice producing a dynamic effect more related to feeling and purpose than profuse and energetic movement of the body— telling us how much the character lives. The expression of emotion is largely through the control and release of breath. The quality known as intensity is the most potent instrument the actor can possess, that is emotional energy in the voice: power under control. The ability to convey emotion through the voice, and control it, is the answer to "ham," which is obvious loud, false vocal expression of feeling. The choice not to ham is a matter of discrimination and taste, but unless the actor has the vocal means, he has only the two alternatives: to ham or to underplay.

Speech and Articulation

Many actors are limited by the nature of their articulation, the way in which they shape and use speech. Middle-class English speech seems to contribute to an essentially tense use of the mouth: a stiff jaw, strangled utterance, and a lack of facial expression: the English personality captured in a manner of speaking. English audiences, however, are subtle and critical judges of social class and education, and something so small as an imperfect diphthong may strike a note of unreality: imagine Edmund in *King Lear* beginning

> Theouw, nature, art my goddess; to thy law
> My services are beound. . . .

There seems little doubt that standard English is the best platform for a versatile actor: that is, spoken English based not on an idea of social class but on purely technical premises: the mechanics of speech. The talented actor of accented or idiosyncratic speech is at once limited to those roles where his vocal mannerisms are credible. Fortunately the theatre can absorb and use such vocal individuality, provided that other criteria of good stage speech are met: clarity, tone, and audibility. Inaudibility may be the fault of sloppy or woolly articulation when the actor is trying to vary pace; inflexible lips and an unagile tongue conspiring to slur and misplace consonants: consider Bohun, QC, from Shaw's *You Never Can Tell*:

> Now lissun to me, yawl of you. I give no wopinion, M'comas, sas
> (Now listen to me, all of you. I give no opinion, M'Comas, as)
>
> ter how far you may yor may notuv committed yerself in the
> (to how far you may or may not have committed yourself in the)
>
> d'reckshun indicated by thi syoung lady. No, don' int'rupt me:
> (direction indicated by this young lady. No, don't interrupt me:)
>
> if she duzzn' marry you she'll marry somebody yelse. That is the
> (if she doesn't marry you she'll marry somebody else. That is the)

slushun nuv the diff'culty yas to her not bearing her father
sname.
(solution of the difficulty as to her not bearing her father's
name.)

The most notable characteristic of Bohun is that he is terrifyingly
articulate: only his powers of speech can show us the ruthless
vigour of his mind, and he is a great actor of the courtroom. The
elisions and intrusive consonants shown could ruin the performance. It is not an over-simplification to say that in this case the
articulation is half the characterization (as indeed it is with Eliza
Doolittle).

Or consider the appalling Lenny, from Pinter's *The Homecoming*:

> Eh, listen, I wonder if you can advise me. I've been having a
> bit of a rough time with this clock. The tick's been keeping me
> up. The trouble is, I'm not at all convinced it was the clock.
> I mean, there are lots of things which tick in the night, don't
> you find that? All sorts of objects, which in the day you
> wouldn't call anything but commonplace. They give you no
> trouble. But in the night any one of a given number of them
> is liable to start letting out a bit of a tick. . . .

The problems of articulation are complicated here. The content
of the speech is the merest pretext for Lenny to chat up Ruth: the
manner is all-important. His glib flannelling is probably delivered
at high speed, or speed has to be related to a sense and emotion
that are ambiguous. The accent is probably Cockney, over which
he has imposed some sort of middle-class accent, with a dash of
American thrown in. The actor can put together the ingredients
of Lenny's character, and then discover that most of the realities
are deeply hidden behind a façade of slickness and shoddy eloquence: that he must show us what Lenny's playing at, and
what he's hiding, through the medium of his speech. All spoken
text needs careful consideration as to how to articulate it. The
experienced actor will possess a polished articulation, skill in
varying it, and a sense of character expressed by speech (if he or
she is a character actor). Jim Dale, in a delightful performance
of that difficult character, Costard, the clown, made ingenious

play with the word "remuneration". He played it as a wondrous word: intoxicated by the sheer SIZE of it, the music as it rolled off the tongue, the grandeur that it gave to the idea of mere WAGES. Just by picking on how to speak one word, he gave us a sharp yokel discovering, and satirizing the language of the powerful.

Actors must possess skill in use and choice of the sounds by which they convey their meaning, using the consonants with precision, and the vowels with musicality. Obvious consonontal weaknesses are sloppy explosives (P,T,K, B,D,G). The sounds S,T, and D can be irritatingly at fault by being sibilant, that is, they have the quality of a hiss or a whistle. The sound L is often swallowed, producing a sound that Clifford Turner exemplified as "miook" (milk). R becomes painfully disruptive when it is turned into a sound resembling "ooh-er". This is only of use as a stage affectation, usually given to heavy swells of East End pawnbrokers. The director is responsible for the spoken quality of his production, so he must demand very high standards of speech, and possess the knowledge and skill to help the actor toward greater clarity.

Tone: Trumpet or Flute

Dramatic speech, especially that which has some poetic quality, must use a variety of notes, sustain a vibrant and interesting tone and deliver words with utter clarity, even if it's speech which departs from the norm. Much of the psychology of character doesn't have to be spelled out: it can be recognized by the way in which a character uses words. One of the causes of displeasure when listening to a play is the overall failure to sustain tone, a most elusive fault: tone being the quality of the actor's sound. Many actors lose their tone when the note in the voice is high or low, and the voice becomes harsh or husky: the sound is ugly and unmusical, in spite of the fact that the actor may be using variety of volume, pitch and tempo. Another failure of the use of tone is when actors are continually sonorous in tragedy, sacrificing meaning for a perfection of tone which approaches the operatic. The only remedy for the director is to listen acutely to the performance from the front and back of the auditorium: there should be no sensation of loudness at the front, nor inaudibility at the back. Correct breathing, and full relaxed use of the resonators produce the voice that is a continuous pleasure to listen to. An audience cannot identify the vocal performance that fails through inconsistencies of tone: they are merely unsatisfied, as one might be when listening to a bore. Equally, they merely recognize a fully resonant voice with the words "What a beautiful voice." As a rider to these remarks, the "voice Beautiful" which is not allied to the other talents of the actor is no more use when acting than beautiful legs or a beautiful face!

The Notes of the Voice

The actor's sound is only interesting when it is varied. This is achieved by variety of volume, pace and timing, and changes of pitch. That is, the number of notes the actor can use. The range of notes is dictated by the actor's vocal cords, and his "ear", the ability to hear different notes. If he has a good ear he can extend his range by practice and use, and increase his expressive possibilities. We all have a range natural to ourselves: we may be a soprano, contralto, tenor, baritone, or bass. The actor must find his range, and develop it. Olivier, when preparing to play Othello, perceived the great musicality of the language, and the qualities and effect of the character, and to meet the needs of the part worked to develop his lower notes. The actor's aim is to sustain a good tone and ease of delivery while using the maximum range of notes. Quite simply, deep notes are sexy and reassuring (see innumerable Hollywood sex-symbols): high notes are tense and dramatic (see innumerable operatic Divas).

Like singers, the actor plays parts that are suitable for his or her voice: Desdemona is a soprano, Cleopatra a contralto. As a consideration for the director, two characters of the same sex who talk to each other a lot should be of slightly different pitch range. Every play has a huge and varied "profile" of musical notes: so has every exchange between characters, and so has every long speech. The director should sharpen his awareness of this varied pattern of pitch by an enthusiasm for Musicals and Opera; how does the MUSICAL drama make its effects on the audience's emotions? Mozart and Rogers and Hammerstein demonstrate the compelling, seductive qualities of the right voice, saying the right things, at the right tempo, at the right pitch.

As the play is a great musical pattern, so is the long speech. It tells us exciting and important things about feelings, ideas and attitudes: suddenly disgorges the depths of the character, makes illuminations and revelations. It must be arrestingly interesting. So the actor and director must get into cahoots pretty soon about its sheer compulsive excitement, its ability to grab the audience. If it's got this, first of all, they'll listen, and probably understand it. So it must have a musical shape, of notes and rhythm, that helps to convey its meaning and feeling, and makes it interesting purely for its sound value. A great speech is rather like a great aria, and it must move, or thrill, as well as inform.

Most actors use too few notes, because most of the dialogue they speak is modern and naturalistic, or because they are type-cast in parts that use their natural range. All dramatic speech is more exciting when the note is varied: consider Brando's remarkable performance in *The Godfather*, like a stoked-down volcano—where the merest shift of half a note spelt DANGER!

Conveying Meaning: Using Inflection

Inflection is the voice in action: its conveyance of meaning and expressiveness. The English language is a superb instrument for the actor, not only for the range of its vocabulary but for its subtlety in use, the varied possibilities which can be given to a form of words by variation of pitch and tempo. Perhaps the most frequently given note by directors is "keep up the inflection." The falling and rising inflections have their own effects: the dropping pitch has a finality about it which terminates an idea, calls for a momentary pause. It is in itself an emphasis, and is often used for the definite statement, the absorption of an idea. The energy of performance, the continuity of thought and feeling is temporarily suspended, and must be lifted again with vigorous attack. The diffident and uncertain actor tends to reveal his lack of conviction by repeatedly allowing either the note or the pace to drop.

The effect is, overall, one of melancholy, and is very infectious; it is a commonplace of rehearsal to find actors picking up each other's pattern of speech and inflection, which is usually given the misnomer of "picking up each other's tone," meaning that pitch and pace over a number of speeches slow down and drop, or become monotonous. This is particularly noticeable in verbal comedy when it's flat, and all the other ingredients of character and relationships have been established. The scene fails to get off the ground, and the remedy is probably the simple one of pace, giving energy, and inflection, giving faster reactions, faster connections and changes of thought. The rising inflection which lifts at the end of a phrase, or line, or speech keeps us listening, and doesn't break the thought. Inflection is a subtle matter, and needs clever choice: consider this passage from *The Way of The World*, Congreve's dazzling comedy of wit and humour. Mirabel and Fainall, for their own amusement, are egging on the egregious Witwould, who is demolishing his friend Petulant with faint praise.

WITWOUD. . . . I can defend most of his faults, except one or two; one he has, that's the truth on't, if he were my brother, I could not acquite him—that indeed I could wish were otherwise.

MIRABEL. Ay, marry, what's that, Witwoud?

WITW. O pardon me—expose the infirmities of my friend,— no, my dear, excuse me there.

FAINALL. What, I warrant, he's unsincere, or 'tis some such trifle.

WITW. No, no, what if he be? 'Tis no matter for that, his wit will excuse that: a wit should no more be sincere, than a woman constant: one argues a decay of parts, as t'other of beauty.

MIRA. Maybe you think him too positive?

WITW. No, no, his being positive is an incentive to argument, and keeps up conversation.

FAIN. Too illiterate.

WITW. That! That's his happiness—his want of learning gives him the more opportunity to shew his natural parts.

MIRA. He wants words.

WITW. Ay; but I like him for that now; for his want of words gives me very often the pleasure to explain his meaning.

FAIN.	He's impudent.
WITW.	No, that's not it.
MIRA.	Vain.
WITW.	No.
MIRA.	What, he speaks unseasonable truths sometimes, because he has not wit enough to invent an evasion.
WITW.	Truths! Ha, ha, ha! No, no, since you will have it,—I mean, he never speaks truth at all,—that's all. He will lie like a chambermaid, or a woman of quality's porter. Now **that . . . IS . . . A FAULT.**

In this passage, the yeast of the comedy is the rising inflection: sometimes on a word—"He's impudent?" with Fainall searching for the right deadly derogatory word—or a phrase; "one argues a decay of parts, as t'other of beauty." A strongly falling inflection on the last phrase will take Witwoud out of the conversation, by giving an emphasis which must be accepted or argued. The one really effective falling inflection would seem to be on the last line, not before, with both pitch and tempo dropping. In the pattern of speech of the entire passage, inflection is of crucial importance: it dictates the pace, the lightness, the laughs, and the final climax.

Another problem of inflection which is very often encountered, particularly in the amateur theatre, is chattiness, overstressing: the inexperienced actor fears that he or she will sound dull, or fail to get their meaning across, so every word that can be stressed is amplified:

> Oh, *where* is it all *gone? What* has become of my *past,* when I was *young, gay,* and *clever* when my *dreams* and *thoughts* were *exquisite,* when my *present* and my *past* were *lighted* up by *hope?* (Andrey in *The Three Sisters.*)

This would seem to be a ludicrously overstated example of overstressing to convey meaning, yet it is typical of the over-enthusiastic novice who has little realization of the possibilities of dramatic speech. The selection of stress words must be carefully done: the word may be stressed by means of pitch, or timing, for example the fractional momentary pause before or after the word, or a slow and delicate speaking of the word itself: or by volume. All this amounts to a melody, a tune of a kind, and over-manipulation could kill the intrinsic musicality. The words emphasized in the example do present an exact sense, but they do it merely by being spoken, with clarity and appropriate feeling. In practice, this speech might work very well in almost a monotone: it's a controlled expression of thought, not an outburst or raving, and perhaps only the words "gone," "exquisite," and "hope" need any quality of emphasis. The more poetic, imaginative, allusive the substance of a speech the larger the pattern of inflection. The words must be trusted to do the work of conveying meaning. Vocal fussiness, over-adornment, dissipates mood or intensity: consider this passage from *Othello*, as spoken by Olivier, a consummate master of inflection:

> Never, Iago. Like to the Pontic sea,
> >   Whose icy current and compulsive course
> Ne'er feels retiring ebb, but keeps due on
> >   To the Propontic and the Hellespont;
> Even so, my bloody thoughts, with violent pace,
> >   Shall ne'er look back, ne'er ebb to humble . . . *love*,
> Till that a capable and wide revenge
> >   Swallow them up.

The speech is spoken, first, with a powerful rhythmic sense: words are stretched like elastic—"Never," "due on," "Even so," "ne'er," "ne'er ebb," "swallow." Changes of pitch are very slight and subtle: it's played at a powerful level of intensity, and the only word really isolated by inflection is "love," after a pause, stammered, nearly whispered. The meaning of the speech, love converting to hate, rage catching fire, is beautifully captured in that one stress and the frame is always rich in tone, utterly clear.

The acquisition of vocal skill, and understanding the paramount importance of voice and speech to the stage actor, takes time, patience and great effort. The demands of the theatre are as exacting in Coward's comedies as in Shakespeare. The exciting developments of the theatre today have rather obscured this necessity, indeed made good speech and a fine voice a secondary consideration for many young actors, in revolt against the theatrical values of a previous generation. The qualities of the means of good acting are timeless, and separate from the philosophy of the age, Personality, intellect, up-to-dateness, sex appeal and physical ease and athleticism are all highly desirable and useful to the actor, but must support this fundamental skill, as important as mastery of the keyboard to the pianist, or control of the ball to a footballer.

Rhythm

"Rhythm" is a vague word, often used by directors, as if it were a quality of tempo that could easily be identified from the text, and then applied to the speaking of the words with magical effect. It is a much more complicated and subtle matter. It cannot be isolated from meaning and mood, tone and volume, and also applies to the physical and mental part of acting—breathing, moving, looking, listening, making gestures. The quality of rhythm must finally pervade a good performance, but first of all must be sought in the text itself.

A dramatic text may indicate a rhythmic structure: that is, a regular metric, poetic form, for example, each line containing the same number of syllables, or the same number of stresses, or even rhymes. Example:

> If music be the food of love, play on,
> Give me excess of it, that surfeiting,
> The appetite may sicken, and so die.
> That strain again! It had a dying fall;
> O, it came o'er my ear like the sweet sound
> That breathes upon a bank of violets,
> Stealing and giving odour!   Enough, no more; . . . .

Ten syllables, five stresses to a line. A lot of the Elizabethan and Jacobean drama uses this mode, which *works*. There are many other unactable or seldom performed plays in different metres, for example the plays of the nineteenth-century romantic poets. There are also plays in poetic language and rhythms of a freer kind, for example Elliot, Fry, Williams and Lorca. Regularity with simplicity of rhythm certainly does power speech along, and like musical theatre helps toward the creation of mood: great climaxes, tranquil, serene, or seductive passages, rich narratives (consider the sheer density and atmosphere of the choruses to *Henry V*): it also has an hypnotic effect on the listener, who "tunes in", mentally, physically, and emotionally. Yet rhythm in a text, useful though it can be, can also have an adverse effect, that of sending the audience into a trance. Consider:

> DE DAH DE DAH DE DAH DE DAH DE DAH,
> DE DAH DE DAH DE DAH DE DAH DE DAH,
> de dah de dah de dah de dah de dah. . . . (etc.)

Sense and feeling are still paramount. Rhythm, in a rhythmic text, is something that FLOATS UP during rehearsal, the repeated speaking of the words, something that gradually asserts itself to the right measure. If the rhythmic quality is put first, as if it were a religious observance, the result will probably be sprouting.

It's there, so it shouldn't be hammered. It's the indestructible skeleton of the words and sense, and if a speech is worth saying, the metre is built in to the sense and feeling. The actor's first target must be not metre, but phrasing for sense, the phrase being the smallest group of words that make sense on their own:

> If music . . . be the food . . . of love . . . play on
> Give me . . . excess of it . . . that surfeiting. . . .

This is not the only way to phrase it, there are several alternatives to choose from. What the actor has to do is say the lines, a lot of times: it's done by feel, not decision. Rhythm is a part of artistic truth, depth of feeling and meaning. It's not music, not an absolute mathematical value, and varies according to the actor, and his or her personality and interpretation.

Back to Orsino: it's a well-known speech, and the first line is often quoted. The Duke is a love-sick, and sometimes slightly comic romantic, but he expresses himself with superb elegance. If high-powered speech reveals character and emotion, this is uttered by an eloquent and cultivated man who relishes the sophistication and finesse of his own feelings and talk. Self-indulgent, to music. So it has a steady pulse, a musicality, and reveals his high sensibilities and his voluptuousness. Consider the effect of phrasing the speech to suggest spontaneous, rational thought: it becomes merely neurotic, and he needs a tranquillizer.

Rhythm in prose speech is much more elusive. There is almost no regularity of stress, and little conscious arrangement of pulse. Rhythm in prose is more a matter of sensing its *elasticity*. Like driving a high-powered car, with subtle gear changes, delicate braking, light steering, and vigorous acceleration: over hills, autostrada, cart-tracks, sand, ice. To find what rhythms exist is a matter of feel more than judgement, as it's even more instinctive than human and dramatic commonsense, and the actor needs to speak the lines a lot, in rehearsal, to somebody, to a tape recorder. Analysis of the form won't help much, as there is no regularity, but constant variation of pulse:

> What am I, Governors both?/ Don't look at it that way./
> I'm one of the undeserving poor: that's what I am./Think
> of what that means/to a man./It means/that he's up agen/
> middle class morality/all the time./If there's anything going,/
> and I put in for a bit of it,/it's always the same story:/
> 'YOURE UNDESERVING;SO YOU CANT HAVE IT.'
> But my needs is as great as the most deserving widow's that
> ever got money out of six different charities in one week for
> the death of the same husband . . . (Doolittle, *Pygmalion*.)

Shaw has chosen to make his philosophical dustman a natural genius of oratory, and his speech fairly swings along, full of sonorities, alliterations, sound sense, but grandeur.

Rhythm is an important dimension which can only emerge when the text and its ideas and feelings are soaked into the actor's bones.

The Actor and Movement

The use of movement for the actor must be based on accurate observation of humankind, and training and development of the body. The stage, more than any other acting medium isolates him, and all physical actions assume a significance as profound as the wordless actor's ability to tell a story, and communicate emotion and feeling, though his is a precise and specialized art, to which few ordinary actors could aspire. Actors vary greatly in their capacity for bodily expressiveness, according to their degree of co-ordination, build and muscularity, and temperament, and, alas, are usually only too ready to become physically typed. Were such limitations of physical possibility to prevail in musical theatre, and opera especially, there would be no heroes and heroines! The object of the actor's use of movement is, however, to transcend bodily limitations as far as possible, and to add to the overall expressiveness of performance. As a dramatic text represents a statement of the utmost economy, so the actor's physical performance must contain nothing extraneous: few actors would insert extra words, or supplementary noises of the Ah Ooh Sure Yeah kind, except by way of suitable reaction. So, certain movements can be justifiably motivated, but are beyond the needs of the play. Much of the bodily training and assistance that the actor needs is the reminder not to dissipitate his energy through insignificant gesture, moves and tensions. As a starting point for performance it is better to be relaxed and wait for spontaneous and truthful action to arise, than to start physically "characterizing" at once. "Gesture" cannot be taught, except in a stylized and mimetic sense, nor can posture, walking or sitting. They can be the subject of experiment in the movement class or rehearsal, but finally emerge from motivation which meets with an expressive response. As with speech, tension and effort are the actor's enemy: the signs vary, and the director must observe them in rehearsal, and help the actor eliminate them: they may be merely the growing pains of performance developing, or a misuse of energy due to the interpretation of the role, for example the actor trying too hard, in tragedy or comedy! The comic idea of an acting novice has been wickedly depicted by the comedian Benny Hill: a wooden figure, with stiff and conspicuous hands, and bunched shoulders, apparently with the coat-hanger still in the jacket; lip-licking, basilisk eyes darting uneasily too and fro. Few actors really present such a grotesque, but even a capable actor can be seen in apparent repose with one hand slightly tensed, twitching his fingers, or with the head slightly too alert: I recently saw a fine actor giving a *tour de force* performance, with one foot relentlessly beating time to the rhythm of the lines. Any uncalled-for tension means get up and go, not in the play, but from it. The object of rehearsal is to achieve a unity of physical action with mental and verbal action, an absolute fusion of all the means of expression. This unity can only finally arise spontaneously, total expression born of intuition, feeling and knowledge, and is liable to be blocked if the actor cannot put himself in a neutral bodily condition.

Creative Movement and Body Control

Training falls into several areas. Development of expressiveness through improvisation of actions and physical states, using the senses: touch, sight, taste, hearing and smell; through mime, conveying a dramatic situation entirely through action and reaction. Here the evidence of the senses can be developed; taking smell as an example, sniffing a flower, with a definition of the object: its size, weight, and fragility. From this follows an expression of the mood evoked, pleasure: the slow inhalation, the smile, finally pricking one's finger on the thorn. This seems, like so much discussion of acting, very obvious and elementary, but it is the quality of undergoing experiences and doing things which constitutes good acting, not the complexity of the stimulus or situation. Paradoxically, acting is mainly about simple things, simply, that is understandably expressed. The problem for the actor is to make us oblivious to the artificial confines of the stage, the relationship between audience and actor, and also to give a true reaction to a fictitious stimulus. Stanislavsky expounds this difficulty, and one solution, in his description of a rehearsal of *The Cherry Orchard*, where Liubov's teacup, unbeknown to the actress, was filled with boiling water: at last she dropped it with utter spontaneity. The physical world of sight, sound, textures, dimensions and sensations must at times be evoked with total accuracy and intensity. Realism, naturalism, demands action and reaction which is utterly credible, however enlarged or amplified it is. Much of the physical action of the naturalistic play is banal, but cannot appear so: the actor tries to distil, perfect and sharpen reaction.

The imagination must be capable of expressing an experience in bodily terms, otherwise the actor becomes purely verbal, and dead from the neck down.

Whatever the physique of the actor, a degree of body control is essential, and central to this is the actor's sense of balance, enabling him to move, sit, rise, handle properties, and adjust to the positioning of other actors. The relationship between actors has something in common with that in a team of acrobats, a response and pliability, especially in an intensely physical medium like farce. As the actor strives for flexibility in speech, giving and accepting cues, speeding or slowing a scene, so with movement: when a move is given a tempo, it assumes a particular significance, full of meaning. Let us consider two examples where the degree of body control is the means of conveying so much. In Act II, Scene 4, of *The Way of the World* Millamant makes her first entrance: well into the play, after a tremendous build-up as the most exquisite and desirable of women. Clearly, before she utters a word, she must live up to the audience's expectations of her, and her entrance is described with care:

MIRABEL.   Here she comes i'faith full sail, with her fan spread
               and streamers out and a shoal of fools for tenders
               ——ha no, I cry her mercy.
MRS FAINALL.   I see but one poor empty sculler, and he tows her
               woman after him. . . .
MILLAMANT.   O I have denied myself airs today. I have walked as
               fast through the crowd——
WITWOUD.   As a favourite just disgraced, and with as few
               followers.

This is a tremendous entrance, with as much disdainful innocence and panache as Marlene Dietrich making her way toward the footlights: perfected nonchalance, absolute control of the costume and props, yet the stateliness of a great beauty. This move has sweep and curve, slowness but energy (Millamant is never listless), like the tide coming in: its tempo is not constant, but subtly varied, ending with a romantic composition which dissolves, with a flick of the fan, into another: here we have a woman who has perfected the art of being a social creature, of raising femininity to a high art. If she hasn't, she could be found in any high street. This is a typical example of a character making an entrance for a calculated effect, yet it has another ingredient, in spite of all Millamant's poise: spontaneity, which peeps through the positively Oriental artifice. Theatre tradition has placed much importance on getting on and off the stage: the dramatic punctuation and change of mood it induces. The dramatist usually contrives to make an effect in this way, though the contemporary actor would regard it as "milking," unless there was an essential and striking dramatic possibility to be achieved. Experienced actors can usually produce an hilarious repertoire of "entrance and exit" business, of which the typical example is the door-knob coming off in the hand, exit up the chimney.

The other move to be considered is the entrance of the second messenger in *The Bacchae*. The character, a slave, enters, delivers a tremendous speech, telling of the death of King Pentheus at the hands of the queen and the Bacchic women, and then leaves —the central dramatic act of the play: climax transposed into narrative. The situation is expected, but the revelation when it comes is terrible beyond imagination, and great tension must be built up to this cathartic speech. What seems to be dramatically relevant is not the character of the messenger, which is not indicated in any way, but the condition of a man transfigured, blasted by an experience of which he must tell, then cease to exist. The idea suggested to the actor was a man emerging from fire, from an atomic holocaust. This he transformed into an entrance of intense effort and slowness: a staring, agonized figure walking like a man under the sea, using all his strength in a supreme effort to get to the audience, and tell his story: total concentration on walking to somewhere. When the entrance was played in more realistic terms, staggering and gasping, it lost its tension and power, perhaps because energy was being lost, not saved.

This is a fairly extreme example of stylization of a move, but both entrances illustrate the necessity for economy, and mastery of the body when movement is trying to convey an entire meaning, mood, and situation. We see two apparent opposites required of the actor in motion: relaxation, ease, poise and balance on the one hand, and shape, control of energy and strength on the other. Each part of the body, head, trunk and limbs can be seen to be an expressive part of the whole instrument, conveying thought, feeling and action respectively. The actor strikes his forehead for memory, his breast for love, and picks up his legs to run: thus we might simplify the use of the body. Above all, economy of action is needed. Nothing must distract from our understanding of movement or gesture. It is better that the actor should eliminate all gesture, and simply concentrate on the internal feeling of energy, and the necessary actions, than wave the arms, gesticulate, and pose with the body. The actor gaining experience will pass through a phase of bodily self-consciousness, when he or she is over-aware of hands, arms and body; as the actor passes beyond the elementary stage of being able to relax and curb excessive movement, so he passes to the state when movement and gesture become the agent of feeling and communicate more simply and truthfully than words.

The Actor's Presentation
Guthrie once described how when directing Edith Evans as the glamorous Hesione Hushabye in *Heartbreak House*, the actress appeared to take no notice of his helpful offerings about meaning, moves, timing, etc., and seemed solely preoccupied with her appearance: costume, hairstyling and make-up. Finally, when rehearsals ended with the director convinced of his total failure, and complete lack of communication with the actress, she appeared, looking magnificent, characteristic, and utterly RIGHT. The moral is, that appearance matters to the actor, and the director overlooks this at his peril: in this case, how the actress looked as the character was all-important to her playing it. During the sixties and seventies when a revolution was happening in the theatre, a vast expansion of means and material, one casualty was *what the actor looked like*. For many years productions went on with the actors looking as if they had just walked in off the street. We can dispense with a theatre building or scenery, but we can't do without the excitement of the actor's appearance. Giles Havergal, of the vigorous and

adventurous Glasgow Citizen's Theatre, says that he looks for interesting-looking actors.

The modern actor is highly trained, versatile yet specialized, and to survive must be highly competitive. The modern theatre presents material about areas of society, morality, work and politics undreamed of two decades ago, yet at the same time it is still a world of glamour, beautiful, glittering and powerful people, innocence, and heroism. Often the actor's first duty is to please and charm, to be the epitome of grace or beauty. In this endeavour the director is the actor's impresario and Svengali. Actors must be encouraged to develop skill in their personal presentation, both on and off stage. This implies having a sense of style in the use of clothes, hair styling, and make-up, sharpening the awareness of the significance of appearances. The look of the character immediately plants an idea in the audience's mind, and if the look is wrong, the actor is struggling unnecessarily to be credible, his first and basic duty.

Since the modern actor is trying to sell his or her talent in an overcrowded profession, he or she must apply their sense of presentation to their offstage appearances, particularly when in pursuit of work and socializing professionally. They must find out what clothes flatter them, how to dress attractively but cheaply: cut and fit are more important than colour, and one cherished expensive item of clothing can make an inexpensive outfit. The director, when casting or interviewing actors often has to make decisive choices between many similar actors, and is likely to engage a tidy looking actor on the assumption that he will be tidy-minded and professional. If the director has a part to play as guide, chairman, and arbiter of a company of actors, he must have their well-being at heart, and where necessary take on the role of manager-cum-coach to a team of sportsmen and women. He must be concerned not only with the development of professional skills, but must also encourage their personal development. Good acting only emerges from whole personalities.

Thus, the actor. No summary of his skills, no guesses about his mind and nature can possibly do justice to his part in the success of theatre. He is second only to the dramatist. The director's attitude to the actor must be founded on this truth, and he must study him with insight and sympathy all his working life, offering him the security of wise advice, intellectual clarity, and help in developing his skill. Above all, enthusiasm: a company of actors is like a frail raft making for the shore: only the spirit of the steersman can land them safely.

5
Moving the Play

Planning the movement and action, the stage pictures and visual images of a play, is one of the most useful and satisfying phases of direction. However much it may change or develop during rehearsal, the director has in his study gone through a process somewhat akin to making a film, telling a story through a series of pictures: sometimes a grand spectacle, sometimes a close-up. The usefulness of this process is because it's thorough, and demands study of the text. Every move, position, grouping and action needs a motivation, arising from the text, from character, or simply the directorial necessity to make things work smoothly. However loose a framework of moves the director may start rehearsal with, his exploration of the text means that he has moved toward that fusion of speech and action that is the play brought to life.

Create your own Moves

Many plays in published forms are "acting editions." It is right that a play which has been performed should have that performance documented: it has become a work of literature containing descriptions of action and movement. However, it is an open invitation to actors and directors to repeat the moves and business of somebody else's production, planned for a different theatre, staging, and actors. A production is unique, an acutely personal matter, relative to those who create it, so the only thing a company can usefully derive from an acting edition is a general impression. The director must start from scratch and create a new production for his actors. Only extreme pressure of time, or total inexperience should make the director resort to doing exactly what it says in the book. It is probable that a director will come up with many similar solutions to the first director of the play. The inexperienced director can afford to study the suggested moves and business in an acting edition, then try to create his own frame of moves for the play. How much time should be given to plotting, or "blocking"? If the director's preparation has been thorough, and the actors are responsive, about a fifth of rehearsal time, assuming say eighty hours of rehearsal. Obviously this will depend on the visual nature of the play, the number of settings, number of actors, and the complexity of the action: *Look Back In Anger* will be simple to block compared with *Julius Caesar*. Some directors, including the very eminent, are known to continue changing moves until the final stages of rehearsal, no doubt for better ones, but the actor finds this very unsettling. Obviously moves will change as rehearsal progresses, but this should only mean that improvements are made, not that the pattern of movement is totally changed. Clearly, every play could be given several effective alternative sets of moves: one of them should be discovered as soon as possible. Most of the general planning of the pattern of movement should be well established by half way through rehearsals.

The moves of a play make a strong statement, and must be motivated by situation, relationship, or emotion: and the motivation must be discovered in the text, or must be in keeping with the action as a whole, and have some dramatic justification. For example, it may be necessary to invent moves to regroup actors in a conversation piece: to this end, tables of drinks, cigarette boxes, windows with ostensibly alluring views are provided to afford pretexts for moving. One picture can become monotonous, and an audience needs change and stimulus to the eye. The object of moving the play is more than the creation of agreeable or dramatic pictures: like good art, the stage picture must have a focus, and the audience must be directed where to look at any time. As the picture must represent some degree of reality, these manipulations of the audience's attention must be unobtrusive. Working out possible moves helps the director to check on his use of the stage: whether he has used moves monotonously, at the same speed and in the same positions; whether he has used the acting area to the full, or generally placed the play too far upstage or downstage; whether he has been too constricted by furniture and staging. A small or over-large stage is particularly challenging to the director, and movement needs careful advance planning. The inexperienced actor also must be planned for: his use of space will be insensitive, and he will be incapable of the adjustments of speed, space and energy in the use of moves which the trained actor accepts from one production to the next.

Movement on the stage is conditioned by theatrical reality: the actors are seen to best advantage whilst movement looks natural, except in deliberate stylization. Many of the conventions of artifice have become redundant: actors may well stand with their backs to the audience, as long as they are not delivering lines where we need to see them: the convention of "cheating" into full face or three-quarter profile when working on the proscenium stage is purely operatic, where the performer must see the conductor. "Masking," though undesirable, is inevitable in naturalism, for example in a crowded scene: not to mask might sometimes result in large semicircular groupings repeated again and again. Every old hand will have certain taboos, such as not moving when speaking, not moving when another actor is speaking, etc. The only criterion for movement is sense and feeling, not tradition. All artistic media are a source of inspiration to the theatre: dance, the use of rhythm, ritual acts, portraits, historic clothing, customs, and artefacts. So much human activity is encompassed by the theatre that all forms and expressions of movement can be of use to the director, as they are to the actor. Finally the director must discover the most interesting, yet economical, way of presenting the physical world of the play.

Large-scale Use of Movement: Realism and Stylization

It is not possible to prescribe rules or a system by which a play can be put into action: possibilities are explored, and a choice made. Let us examine some situations from two plays, and the possibilities they contain for movement. First, *The Caucasian Chalk Circle*, by Bertolt Brecht.[1] The play is a Marxist didactic parable about ownership and justice, yet so much more: rich in humour, indignation, polemic, debate, it uses the ways and means of total theatre to communicate the story of Grusche and her adoption of the Governor's child, and Azdak, the picaresque

---

[1] The passages following are quoted by permission from Bertolt Brecht, *The Caucasian Chalk Circle* from *Parables for the Theatre*, translated by Eric Bentley. University of Minnesota Press, Minneapolis, © 1948, Eric Bentley.

village clerk who becomes a judge. The play is a great panorama of human activity, containing scenes of high emotion, satire, adventure, spectacle, and didactic delivery of fact. It becomes apparent that almost every theatrical means may be used to convey the rich experience of the play: story-telling, pantomime, song, pictorialism, naturalism, stylization: because it's Brecht, the play has the vivid animation of a strip cartoon; there are many scenes, to make us aware that it's a theatrical experience we're undergoing, and in those scenes exists almost every possibility for the use of movement. The following brief excerpts must be examined for their hypothetical moves: first, motivated moves with a reason of story or character; next, director's moves, to make the action work, or create atmosphere or mood, or enhance the scene visually; finally reactive moves, of response, or involuntary moves expressive of the character's psychology. Obviously each move is only one possibility of many.

From Scene ii:

(*Two soldiers (Ironshirts) are trudging along a highway.*)

CORPORAL. You'll never amount to anything, Blockhead! Your heart's not in it. Your senior officer sees it in little things. Yesterday, when I made the fat gal, I admit you grabbed her husband as I commanded, and you did kick him in the stomach, but did you enjoy doing it like a loyal private? Or were you just doing your duty? I've kept my eyes on you, Blockhead. . . . I forbid you to limp! . . . You limp just to show me you don't like marching. . . . SING!

Two splendid comic military monsters: they must be kept marching in the middle of the stage, on the spot; no point in moving them around the stage, it's the act of marching that matters. Corporals and enlisted men haven't changed: the corporal is a strutting man of iron, Blockhead a sloppy rifle-dropper. Almost Morecambe and Wise, but they are a real threat to Grusche: they are after the Governor's child, and rape is the corporal's speciality. During the following scene, they could be kept on stage: the tension of a sequence of scenes is mounting until Grusche makes her escape over the bridge:

CORPORAL.   Christ, how am I to get my hands on the Governor's bastard with a fool like you!

STORY-TELLER.   When Grusche Vashnadze came to the river Sirra, the flight grew to much for her, the helpless child too heavy.... (*Grusche stops in front of a farm.*)

Here the technique of transition from one scene to the next becomes very fluid, a change of lighting, sound effects, and Grusche's weary staggering entrance: a solitary, touching, shapeless figure. It might be effective to punctuate the marching of the soldiers with a distant, relentless drum-tap, which never ceases till she has escaped from them: however, during the narrative above they must be moved from the centre of the stage, perhaps by countermarching them on the spot, and marching them upstage to centre, where with their backs to us they tramp rhythmically and silently. Never out of the sight of the audience, their rhythmic and mechanical marching pervades the scene. Grusche arrives. Upstage, at one side. A long move downstage gives her the chance to use it, to show her ragged exhaustion. She pauses, wipes her head and face, heaves the heavy child on to her shoulder again, and staggers downstage. The peasant woman, preoccupied, enters on the other side of the stage: Grusche freezes, clutches the child tightly to her to silence it. As the woman enters the "house" Grusche relaxes her hold on the child. He's wet his pants.

Here we have movement with naturalistic motivation and stylization mixed: actors being realistic in action, but not in relation to scenery (Grusche and the peasant woman) and two using stylized action and positioning (the two soldiers).

Let us now examine a more complex scene: the opening of the play, using a crowd and highly individualized but briefly seen characters some of whom must be memorable in spite of a short appearance. The scene is the city square in the capital. The opulent governor, his family and their hangers-on, and his rival, a war-lord prince, enter in a procession to go to church, and are surrounded by a mass of starving beggars. Revolution is in the air and we have in a brief scene to create an exotic and fantastic atmosphere, vivid contrasts between magnificence and mutilated poverty. A symbiosis of movement, effects and sound must be evolved, with the moves as the starting point. The play derives from the parable of the Chalk Circle, and there's a feel of Oriental theatre about it. The stage has a huge gateway upstage right, a great door to the church up left, both of which arches could be trucked and serve as architectural bare bones for the rest of the play, the framework for huts, houses, bridges, etc.

The story-teller speaks:

> In olden times, in a bloody time,
> There ruled in a Caucasian city—
> Men called it the city of the damned—
> A governor.
> His name was Georgi Abashwilli.
> He was as rich as Croesus
> He had a beautiful wife
> He had a healthy child.
> No other governor in Grusinia
> Had so many horses in his stable
> So many beggars on his doorstep
> So many soldiers in his service
> So many petitioners in his courtyard.
> Georgi Abashwilli—how shall I describe him?
> He enjoyed his life.
> On the morning of Easter Sunday
> The governor and his family went to church.

During this steadily building narrative, we can suggest movement by introducing the rhythm of the procession soon to appear: two rhythms: the rocking fluidity of the governor's wife and the strong rhythm of the governor. The scene erupts. A gong might be used to punctuate the shift in the scene. A great dusty crew of beggars, (all eight of them in the average production) roar through the upstage arch preceding the governor: they hop on crutches, jump, kneel, grovel, shove and implore, as the governor stalks loftily on:

> Mercy! Mercy! Your Grace! The taxes are way up, we can't pay!
> I lost my leg in the Persian war, where can I get. . . .
> My brother is innocent, Your Grace, there's been a misunderstanding. . . .

—The child is starving in my arms!
—We plead for our son's discharge from the army, our last
   remaining son!
—Please, Your Grace, the water inspector takes bribes.

The soldiers, with whips, clear the crowd; a lot more ad lib.
howling and shouting in the same vein is needed; from whirling
circles, the moves of the crowd turn to short, unobtrusive melting
from the centre; as the crowd moves away, they reveal the
governor's wife, surrounded by her retinue: a pause, and she
minces forward, her useless hands held out like dragonflies on
either side of her: the fingernails are ten inches long. Another
pause, followed by comedy: every head turns toward the arch,
a whisper starts: the child! Two doctors, smooth quacks, advance,
followed by a grand, wobbling bassinet, pushed by the head nurse.
More free and encircling movement of the crowd, who can range
about at random if the other actors are observing their fixed
lines of movement very accurately.

The Child!
I can't see it, don't shove so hard!
—God bless the child, Your Grace!

STORY-TELLER. For the first time on that Easter Sunday, the
people saw the Governor's heir.
Two doctors never moved from the noble child,
apple of the Governor's eye.
Even the mighty Prince Kasbeki bows before it at
the Church door.

The fat prince is a monster figure, a gigantic creature clad in
armour, a one-man war machine. Brecht seems to intend him to
be both ridiculous and sinister, and he should have the dignity of
Oliver Hardy or W. C. Fields as he advances on Little Michael:
the politician doing the baby-kissing routine.

The diagram on page 76 will clarify the positioning of the scene,
the arrowed lines showing the track of the moves.

The confines of any stage will hardly permit of a procession,
unless the moves are planned in circles: it would seem sensible
to take the principal characters of the Governor, his adjutant,
and their retinue round the stage several times. Certainly to

improvise the scene without some pre-planning would probably fail to provide the exact quality of sound and silence, energy and tension, straight lines and curves which direct the audience where and when to look. Needless to say, this example, like all the other scenes discussed, is simply one way of realizing it: the choreography, the theatricality of the scene must come from the director's interpretative idea of the play.

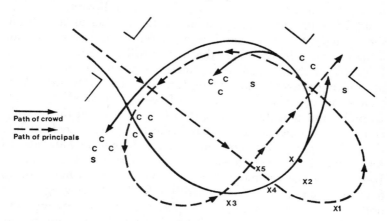

Fig 2 S, *soldiers; C, crowd; 1, Governor; 2, Governor's wife;*
3, fat Prince; 4, pram, nurse; 5, 6, doctors

Moves and Mood

Let us look at another crowd scene from the same play, where a very different quality of movement might be effective: small and naturalist moves, as opposed to large stylization. Grusche, to protect herself and the child, and acquire some papers, takes on a nominal husband, a draft-dodger, ostensibly a sick man about to die. Respectable widowhood must be paid for: Jussup's mother is anxious to sell his potential as a husband before he kicks the bucket, and a wedding with music, eats, and a boozy monk to conduct it is arranged. The scene has a lot in common with North Country farce.

STORY-TELLER.   The bridegroom was lying on his deathbed when
                  The bride arrived.

The bridegroom's mother was waiting at the
door,
Telling her to hurry.

MOTHER-IN-LAW.   Quick! Quick! or he'll die on us before the
wedding!

As the scene is staged, it takes place in a wretched hut: they are
poor peasants. At one side is a bed, with Jussup lying doggo on
it, feigning near death. Grusche, her brother Lavrenti, and the
child Michael enter, dragged in by the mother-in-law. While
she wrangles about the child, and Lavrenti tries to conceal him,
Grusche stares in horror at the totally still invalid. Only a few
feet separate them. A crowd of sanctimonious neighbours sidle in,
murmuring prayers, and bowing formally and awkwardly. They
have come out of curiosity, and to free-load the food and drink.
In bulky and shapeless clothes, they line the walls of the hut, like
chickens on a perch. Two men make for Jussup, to help him
through his part of the ceremony. All exchange formal and absurd
bows, the monk reels toward the bed, Grusche kneels beside
Jussup, and the ceremony begins. Jussup's friends haul him to
a sitting position, like seconds with a K.O.'d heavyweight, and
nod his head for him when a response is not forthcoming. The
whole feel of the scene is one of tightly packed humanity, sweaty
proximity, elbows nudging ribs: no grace or dignity, like a litter
of pigs. Yet they are ridiculously genteel, edging round each other
like guests at a cocktail party.

MOTHER-IN-LAW.   Sit yourself down, please, and have some cakes.

Everybody roosts, crammed together, on the floor. Though they
are clumsy-looking and brutal characters, they have a code of
party manners, and whilst they eat cakes in their hands, they
lick their fingers delicately: bottles are passed too and fro, the
scene becomes ever more lively, dancing begins, an old man
sings an obscene song, the monk makes an indiscreet and bawdy
speech and the mood rapidly develops into a blurred whirl.
Finally, one move changes the scene: Jussup, infuriated by the
guests guzzling, sits up, like Lazarus:

How many more cakes are you going to stuff
down their throats?
D'you think I can shit money?

His revival creates panic, and there is a stampede for the door: howls and shouts, women trampled underfoot, the monk making his exit on somebody's back. The scene is straight out of Breughel, many highly individualized characters in a crowded canvas: the sheer lack of physical freedom, the discomfort and awkwardness of the scene is very near to farce; the circumstances are very different from the intention of the characters.

Movement and Truth

The naturalistic play, with a high degree of realism, a small cast of highly developed characters, and longer, more detailed relationships, needs a freer approach to blocking. Whilst the same conditions apply to moves and their motivation, the effectiveness of the play depends on subtle lifelikeness, with contrivance and theatricality reduced to a minimum. The layout of the stage is usually realistic in the use of stage furniture, and the physical relationship of one character to another, and of characters to their environment, needs much less pre-planning: it will develop during rehearsal. To prejudge the moves too rigidly is to assume too much about the characters, the actors, and their interaction. The actors must feel, realize, and produce spontaneous movement in scenes of subtle exchange of emotion. A loose but commonsense arrangement of moves can be given, just to get things started. Picture composition becomes less important, spectacle irrelevant.

Let us examine a scene of naturalism, and how moves might evolve. The scene is from Arthur Miller's *Death of a Salesman*,[1] a play that could be described as prosaic tragedy: Miller describes it as "what happens to a man when he loses the strings of life." The play examines the life and mind of Willy Loman: his decline and failure, and his relationships with his family, friends, and employers leading up to the time of his death. The play is profoundly concerned with the ethics of a materialistic, success-worshipping society. It uses a composite set, representing many locales, and moves freely in time over twenty years: some scenes are seen with the distorted vision of Willy, but the general effect is of realism, and the ordinariness of family life. The theatricality

---

[1] The following passages are quoted by permission from *Death of a Salesman*, available in *Collected Plays* by Arthur Miller, published by Secker & Warburg, © Arthur Miller, 1949.

is in the play's construction and form, not in its texture: the result is much more of a documentary case-history than a metaphor. This scene is set in Willy's kitchen, late at night. He is sliding into derangement: out in the garden, crazily planting seed, lost in hallucinatory conversation with his long-dead brother Ben. Linda, his wife, sits in the living room, and suffers in tortured patience. His sons, Biff and Happy, men approaching middle age, return after an evening of booze and women. They have stood Willy up, leaving him to fend for himself in a restaurant, his mind tottering.

> (*The light rises gradually on the kitchen, which is empty. Happy appears at the door of the house, followed by Biff. Happy is carrying a large bunch of long-stemmed roses. He enters the kitchen, looking round for Linda. Not seeing her, he turns to Biff, who is just outside the front door, and makes a gesture with his hands, indicating "Not here, I guess." He looks into the living room and freezes. Inside, Linda, unseen, is seated, Willy's coat on her lap. She rises ominously and quietly and moves toward Happy, who backs up into the kitchen, afraid.*)

HAPPY.   Hey, what're you doing up? (*Linda says nothing but moves toward him implacably.*) Where's pop? (*He keeps backing to the right, and now Linda is in full view, in the doorway of the living room.*) Is he sleeping?

LINDA.   Where were you?

NOTE. Linda advancing, Happy backing away. It must be a long move: tension must develop. Linda moves steadily, Happy skips away like a retreating boxer. If Biff moves before Happy's next speech, he takes the focus off them: better to keep him bunched and still outside the door.

HAPPY.   (*Trying to laugh it off.*) We met two girls, mom, very fine types. Here, we brought you some flowers. (*Offering them to her.*) Put them in your room, ma. (*She knocks them to the 'floor at Biff's feet. He has now come inside and closed the door behind him. She stares at Biff, silent.*)

NOTE. Biff's follow-up. Biff is behind Linda, and she faces Happy, having pursued him. She must knock the flowers from Happy's hand to Biff's feet, and interrupt Happy's line "I want you to have some flowers" by turning abruptly from him to face Biff.

HAPPY. Now what'd you do that for? Mom, I want you to have some flowers——

LINDA. *(Cutting Happy off, violently to Biff.)* Don't you care whether he lives or dies?

HAPPY. *(Going to the stairs.)* Come upstairs, Biff.

NOTE. Happy's cross is most effective in the pause, following Linda's question. If he crosses behind Linda he can play the line "come upstairs, Biff" *sotto voce*. Biff's fierce reply leaves him hovering upstage of them, easing their subsequent cross.

BIFF. *(With a flare of disgust, to Happy.)* Go away from me! *(To Linda.)* What do you mean, lives or dies? Nobody's dying around here, pal.

LINDA. Get out of my sight! Get out of here!

BIFF. I wanna see the boss.

LINDA. You're not going near him!

BIFF. Where is he? *(He moves into the living room, Linda follows.)*

NOTE. Biff moves rapidly, after a pause: he races round the house, with Linda following up fast.

LINDA. *(Shouting after Biff.)* You invite him to dinner. He looks forward to it all day ——*(Biff appears in his parent's bedroom, looks round and exits.)*—— and then you desert him there. There's no stranger you'd do that to!

NOTE. "There's no stranger you'd do that to" elicits no reply: Linda turns slowly back into the kitchen: Happy's soft-soap speech which follows seems to motivate some move on her part. It might be best for her to walk past Happy, turning back to him on "get out of here." Biff re-enters: both of them are now facing Linda.

HAPPY. Why? He had a swell time with us. Listen, when I —— *(Linda comes back into the kitchen.)*—— desert him I hope I don't outlive the day!

LINDA. Get out of here!

HAPPY. Now look, mom. . . .

LINDA. Did you have to go to women tonight? You and your lousy rotten whores! *(Biff re-enters the kitchen.)*

HAPPY. Mom, all we did was follow Biff around trying to cheer him up! *(To Biff.)* Boy, what a night you gave me!

LINDA.   Get out of here, both of you, and don't come back! I don't want you tormenting him any more. Go now, get your things together! (*To Biff.*) You can sleep in his apartment. (*She starts to pick up the flowers and stops herself.*) Pick up this stuff, I'm not your maid any more. Pick it up, you bum, you! (*Happy turns his back in refusal, Biff slowly moves over, and gets down on his knees, picking up the flowers.*)

NOTE. Linda kneels to pick up the scattered flowers: then stops herself: the action should happen in a pause, after "you can sleep at his apartment." She stands up, in silence. There is a further short pause before Happy turns his back on her. If he walks away, it looks as if he's provoking her. She looks from Happy to Biff. Another pause: he moves to the flowers: pauses, then kneels. Not till then does she speak again.

LINDA.   You're a pair of animals! Not one, not another living soul would have had the cruelty to walk out on that man in a restaurant!
BIFF.   (*Not looking at her.*) Is that what he said?
LINDA.   He didn't have to say anything. He was so humiliated he nearly limped when he came in.
HAPPY.   But mom, he had a great time with us——
BIFF.   (*Cutting him off violently.*) Shut up! (*Happy goes upstairs without a word.*)

NOTE. Who looks at whom? Happy's bluffing, Biff is really feeling sore at Linda's vituperation, Linda's worrying about Willy, and we should probably be looking at her. Happy gawps at her: "But mom" brings him towards her, Biff's "Shut up" sends him off, a long fast move. If Linda speaks before the reverberations of his exit die away, we lose the tension.

LINDA.   You! You didn't even go in to see if he was all right!
BIFF.   (*Still on the floor in front of Linda, the flowers in his hand; with self-loathing.*) No. Didn't. Didn't do a damned thing. How do you like that, heh? Left him babbling in a toilet.
LINDA.   You louse. You. . . .
BIFF.   Now you hit it on the nose! (*He gets up, throws the flowers in the wastebasket.*) The scum of the earth, and you're looking at him!
LINDA.   Get out of here!

NOTE. "Now you hit it on the nose!" Biff rises. Throws in the flowers before the line "the scum of the earth. . . ." Throwing the flowers after the line is harsher, more dismissive. He wants her co-operation, and must get to Willy, so the action is minimized, taking the steam out of the mood.

BIFF.   I gotta talk to the boss, Mom. Where is he?
LINDA.   You're not going near him. Get out of this house!
BIFF.   (*With absolute assurance, determination.*) No. We're going to have an abrupt conversation, him and me.
LINDA.   You're not talking to him! (*Hammering is heard from outside. Biff turns toward the noise.*)
LINDA.   (*Suddenly pleading.*) Will you please leave him alone?

NOTE. The fragile Linda moves between Biff and the door: her attempt to stop him is to prevent him seeing Willy, motivated by the desire to protect Willy from humiliation: she can't stop him, and sags, her hands over her face.

Motivated, instinctive, and expressive movement are all present in this short scene, and it is impossible to consider the movement divorced from speech and timing: they all contribute to mood and meaning. Every angle of the head, gesture of impulse and attempt at self-control become significant in this atmosphere of tension and heightened emotion, and movement must grow from within, from feeling and understanding. This evolution is a delicate matter, and any "staginess" screams its untruthfulness at us. Not only must movement be expressive of mood and situation, but capture character: Linda has perhaps the stamina of a skinny sparrow, fierce yet fragile: Happy clowns and kids, lazy and posturing. Biff's one-time athleticism has turned into muscle-bound weariness, hunched tension reflecting his inner struggle to break free from the image Willy has cast him in.

Relating Moves to Staging

Let us try to summarize the basic principles of positioning, grouping, and movement, relative to the type of stage and setting. A series of tableaux, however pleasing, is not moving the play if positioning and movement do not support the intention of the acting. First, the proscenium stage. Entrances must be carefully positioned in relation to the audience: an upstage entrance provides an obvious strong entrance, especially if it faces the audience. Its purpose is negated if the arrangement of furniture prevents a follow-up, coming downstage, so whatever furniture is placed on the stage it must be spaced to allow an avenue of five feet or so. Entrances downstage on either side deliver the actor in profile: on a large stage, using a box setting, this means extensive moves in a rather inexpressive position, negotiating all the furniture. Obviously, such a position for a door should only be used when a play demands it, since it means pushing furniture upstage, together with the realistic action. An upstage diagonal entrance is probably the most effective position for a door or entry, if the realism of such details matters. When planning the layout, the traffic routes of the actors, large articles of sitting furniture should not be placed side by side across a small stage, for example a sofa and an armchair: they will, allowing for reasonable spacing, form a barrier some sixteen feet wide, effectively cutting the stage into an upstage and downstage area. A very rudimentary principle might be to draw a line along either diagonal of the stage, and set furniture across it: thus the actors' eyeline is toward the downstage centre of the stage, and the stage is left reasonably unencumbered. The naturalistic play must, while cheating the action to make it viable to the audience, look as realistic as necessary: blank side walls, with the action isolated in the middle, need to be used: the inevitable side table and windows provide logical reasons for moving to the sides of the stage. Equally, the huge stage can have the bounds of a reasonably-sized room set by a carpet, or by large furniture: somehow we must not get the impression of over-large rooms, of the actors bounding about to use the set to the full. Important furniture must have sufficient space all round it, so that the actor can move easily to sit down, or move about: the area by a scenic door needs to be completely clear, on the assumption that several actors may need to be near it at any given time. A ground plan of furniture on the set will reveal how easy it is to move actors on (1) either diagonal; (2) from side to side, upstage and downstage; (3) round each important piece of furniture, and (4) round the periphery of the acting area.

Focus and Dominance

The actor upstage, or facing away from the audience is less audible: and though in a "dominant" position, is only so if reasonably close to them. The dominant position, at the upstage apex of a triangle (beloved of the great actor managers) is monotonous if assumed to be the correct place for all the most important utterances: any part of the stage can be the point of focus, if the other characters on stage are clearly seen to be looking or listening—if the audience's eye has been directed there. Clearly, of two characters alone on stage, one can be the focus of attention when necessary, by the attention of his fellow actor, whether sitting, standing or lying down. Separation also draws the eye to the actor: where, for example, a character must dominate a crowd scene, he can be isolated from the main group, or positioned on a higher level. The theatre of Shakespeare's time provided an in-built strong position with its upstage balcony. Focus would seem to be more important than excessive realism, and movement must never seem fussy: the director's aim should be to give the minimum necessary moves: extreme economy of action, even if it means abandoning half the moves given. Blocking becomes very complex when on the thrust stage or in-the-round area: the point of focus is in a three-dimensional pattern, not a point in a picture. What is gained in intimacy with the audience is paid for in extra movement, and a degree of contrivance. Wherever an actor is placed, he or she will be in profile to some of the audience, or facing away from others: the intimacy of presence or facial expression will be lost. The director's remedy is to turn the actor on the spot; this is possible during a long speech, or if the feeling of the line suggests it, but must be avoided if stillness would be more effective. Too many moves should be avoided, simply to ensure that all of the audience get fair do's, as one would avoid "frontal" playing in the proscenium theatre. If the stage is thought of as several flexible areas, large or small as needed, scenes can be planned for the North, South, East, or West axis, with large spectacular episodes occupying the whole stage. This means that the audience at least see some parts of the play with the fullest degree of intimacy, and all scenes are played for the right spatial relationship. The entrance aisles of an in-the-round area are invaluable for positioning actors on the periphery, where they don't obscure the view for one unfortunate member of the audience. Duologues, intimate scenes, can be stiller, if there is some gain from the closeness of the actors. A competition meant to be viewed from any angle needs constant adjustment, but must not be a problem for the actor, who has other problems and considerations apart from the moves.

The importance of movement to the play must not be underestimated. It is an organic part of the acting, far more than a mere means of giving visual interest to the play. Before starting the process of rehearsal, the director must ask himself "How much of this story is told by word, how much implied by action?" When an answer to this question begins to appear, the play is on its way to proper realization for the stage.

6
Shaping the Play: The Process of Rehearsal

Let us look more closely at the rehearsal process, the most important period of the director's work, when the play gains an extra dimension from the actors. To begin with, we must make some general considerations about audiences, for whom the whole enterprise is undertaken. It would seem that the experience of theatre is largely emotional, and that a large group of people in a theatre is functioning on a lower intellectual level than the intelligence of its individual members. As theatre is a ritual enactment of human life, it would appear to induce emotion, whether of laughter or tears, without the consequences of actual events, and has generally worked in creating feeling, with thought about the events of a play following after the experience.

The Audience: Thinking or Feeling?

In the twentieth century certain innovatory figures have exerted an influence on the theatre by trying to change the way in which the audience react to the play, most notably Brecht and Artaud. Briefly, Brecht set out to establish the "Alienation effect," whereby the audience should be made more objective about the information conveyed in the play. To achieve this end, Brecht required that their emotional involvement with fictitious characters and a fictitious situation should be rudely interrupted; that didactic, factual information should be interpolated into the stream of the play; that the illusion of sustained characterization should be frequently broken (as, for example, Grusche chucking the "baby" into the wings after a scene of tender maternal behaviour) with the actor "demonstrating" the character, offering it up to be judged by the intellect, not identified with. Artaud, for his — part, conceived of a more sensuous experience than the theatre usually offers: by means of images, incantations, acrobatics, light and colour, to approach an audience on a less literary, less verbally coherent, more instinctual level; to present a theatre to be understood at the profoundest core of being, not with the intelligence.

The effect of both these experiments is profound, and traces of their articles of faith are to be found in the work of many contemporary dramatists. However, though we theorize about the nature of the audience, their reactions remain unpredictable. The appreciation of comedy would appear to be a matter of intelligence, yet a feeling is induced—of escape, joy, well-being. The act of laughter releases tensions: much of the stuff of comedy involves suffering—somebody else suffering. To repeat the old axiom, comedy is tragedy happening to somebody else. We cannot assume that a laughing audience is in a state of detachment, with its sense of the ludicrous delicately poised: on the contrary, it is often in a state of glee at the vicarious distresses of the mugs or braggarts who are the central figures: comedy would appear to be a series of acts of violence, either self-inflicted or from without: from, man, woman, Fate or God. This is not to claim that the reaction to comedy is merely a cruel one, but we cannot ignore a certain healthy animal element. Surely comedy, like tragedy, is a ritual enactment of disaster of a lesser kind, from physical injury (the custard pie), to spiritual hurt (the snub). The difference from tragedy is in the human reaction: not noble, heroic, elevated, but sneaky, sensible, realistic. Man will live to fight another day: transcendence has been ducked, laurels are too heavy. The plot of much comedy seems to make little demand on the intelligence, though the ideas may: the characters may be familiar stereotypes, the put-upon-man, the woman whose virtue is in peril, the wit, the boaster, the pompous. Round qualities of character, shallow or profound, may be woven gags which are verbal or active, offering us various levels of enjoyment. Clearly comedy engages our feelings, even when using the most hackneyed methods, and different audiences will enjoy differing experiences, from banana skins to wit. That comedy has a moral seems an inevitable conclusion, but like the message of tragedy, it can only be understood after the event. The audience should not be asked to be very agile mentally, or memorize too many facts: they can be asked to listen and concentrate. We should avoid presenting them with too much at the same time, for example visual metaphors, or significant action while listening to dialogue, unless they support and complement each other. Action and word must not result in two meanings delivered at once. Even a sophisticated audience cannot comprehend a confused message.

At the other end of the scale to audience indigestion is boredom. Its chief cause is vocal monotony, not a boring text. English actors have been enlivening boring plays and investing them with interest for decades. As music sustains our interest with a contrast of voices of varying timbre and range, so a cast of actors give variety of sound, interesting and pleasing in itself. A small range of notes is inexpressive and unexciting: a regularity of rhythm positively soporific; badly acted Shakespeare can send an audience to sleep. The director must seek in the text of a play a vocal shape, something akin to a large and varied work of music, and try to develop it parallel with the actor's performances: vocal climaxes, and anticlimaxes; arias, recitatives, duets. In the best of dramatic writing the dramatist tries to match the form, the verbal shape, to the content: Edward Albee, in *A Delicate Balance*, describes Tobias's outburst as an "aria," and offers suggestions for its vocal shape, loud, soft, slow, fast. As a single speech has a dimension in sound, so has the whole play. Energy is not always expressed in a regular, rhythmic pulse, but in a surge and ebb. Feeling and meaning are the key to what evolves in the way of varied tempo, varied volume. Only lengthy digestion by the director, an insight into the play which is almost instinctive, can reveal the contours of the vocal pattern, when he may ask for "that passage faster," "that speech more quietly." The audience's attention is manipulated by tension, as a comedian takes a pause before a punch-line, or tops a laugh with another gag: tension is built, released, and built up again. Variety, of volume, pace, the use of pause, are all the technical means by which the audience's attention may be controlled by the actor: the most fundamental instrument in the actor's hand is surprise, revelation. The method chosen for telling the story is important: the response is almost childlike.

Visual monotony is like vocal monotony: a continuous similarity of picture means that all images mean the same, or are irrelevant; acting in the centre of the stage, or repeated large groupings, or dull colouring, flat lighting, an absence of Visual contrast, are unemotional, unstimulating. Even the most stern Brechtian is going to seek to invest the scene with a visual reality for its duration, before reminding us that we are watching the process of theatre. Proper consideration of the audience means an adjustment of the director's priorities. He is directing for his author, his actors, and his audience and, last of all, for himself. Whatever happens in rehearsal has no significance unless shared with the audience. How to make that communication most effectively demands a knowledge of what they like, what they need, what they can understand. A play may not immediately be to an audience's liking: it is a mutual exchange, not a mere gratification in exchange for the price of a ticket. The spectator can be asked to participate with feeling and intelligence. "Tired Businessman's Theatre," "Boulevard Comedy," "Coach Party Shows" bow to the demands of the least intelligent part of the audience, The slick, glossy commercial entertainment has great virtues, great charm, but must be presented with the same purposeful attitude as the classical repertoire.

The Pace of Rehearsal

Rehearsal must use time efficiently. The preliminary analysis of the play will reveal something about how much rehearsal is needed for each scene. This will depend on the acting problems: the amount of discussion or clarification needed, the quality of emotion, the difficulty of speaking, performing moves and business, the number of actors involved. A short crowd scene, with fifty words of dialogue from ten actors, may take longer to rehearse than a six-page duologue. A full-length play should be rehearsed for at least ninety hours, but seldom is. A musical, a play with special needs of movement, costume, song and complex scenes needs even longer, anything up to one hundred and fifty hours, which would allow spare time for recapping, for individual rehearsal, or for continuing rehearsal when things are developing fruitfully. The actor must always break from rehearsal with a sense of something achieved, or an objective to be met at the next rehearsal, so the rehearsal schedule needs to be flexible. The schedule should, ideally, consist of the specified scene to be rehearsed, the actors needed, and the time, but of course rehearsal is not a factory for processing plays: it may be necessary to call an actor in to see the scene which precedes his. All actors in a cast should be got together from time to time to see and discuss work in progress, especially the young actor, who is learning from the more experienced, and the amateur, who has a less highly developed sense of concentration. Mutual enthusiasm is a vital quality of good rehearsal.

Though different plays make varied demands, for example deep study of the text before any action can be imagined, at some stage fairly early on the play should be blocked, or plotted. As moves will change during rehearsal, this should be enough to put the play into action, and give the actor a little initial help. The significant part of rehearsal begins when this is completed, so all the actor needs at the blocking stage is a general understanding of the physical style, and a picture of the stage in his mind. Directors are varied in their ideas about when the text should be known: the play itself may demand that the actors know the text before they can rehearse properly. A French farce, for example, may have fragmentary and prosaic dialogue, and an immense amount of action and business, and need to be rehearsed with the greatest freedom, so books need to be discarded as soon as possible. Coward demanded of his actors that they should come to rehearsal knowing the lines, and it is understandable that polished comedy, relying on good casting and expertise does not require the actor to delve into the subconscious. Most directors of experience will expect books to be down halfway through rehearsal, even if it's *Waiting for Godot*. Bitter experience has taught them that it is fatal to indulge the actor who is lazy about learning, since the other actors suffer. The continuing process of rehearsal can only be given a loose form: so much depends on what is developing. A play need not be rehearsed in the acts in which it is written, but rather in groups of scenes that relate to each other in continuity, either of action or character development—units that have an overall objective, and some degree of unity in themselves. The actor cannot absorb too much verbal or demonstrated instruction at any one time, so perhaps it is advisable to work through a scene about three times, interspaced with comment, encouragement and discussion, and then allow the ideas to germinate. Certainly the director must never press the actor for a finished, definitive result in the early stages.

Giving and Taking

What is the balance between director and actor in rehearsal? If the director is the most knowledgeable member of a company, the result can be complete manipulation of the actor, a series of performances as he or she would interpret them. Many a director wonders why their Herculean efforts with a group of novice actors have produced so stilted a result: unless the traffic is two-way, with something creative coming from the actor, acting will never happen.

John Neville at one time opined that perhaps the director was unnecessary if the actor's creativeness could be put in the context of a mutually critical and helpful company; this is a fair point given a fine ensemble of actors, but the average actor has little chance to work in this ideal way, and needs the director to fill the role of critic, adviser, and arbitrator. The actor, however, any actor, has a responsibility for his own performance, and must exercise it. Such is his temperament that he will quite often expect to be excited, cajoled, adored and bullied at various moments of rehearsal, but this cannot happen throughout. A director should make it known that he expects the actor to be creative in his province, whilst he, the director, provides the guidance to the exploratory process. Discussion is more enjoyable than the gritty process of digging out a performance, so the actor will discuss at inordinate length either to delay the moment of truth, or for the joy of debate! Olivier has said that he would sooner go through a scene eight times than discuss it: rehearsal is the improvisation round the text itself when something spontaneous must emerge from the actor. A clear concept of objectives is necessary, but it needn't contain all the possibilities of the scene: a lot is discovered by the accident of rehearsal. If a scene excites the imagination of actor or director, that seems to be the time to pursue it. The discussion that arises can be very revealing to the director about the actor's thought process: the ideas that stimulate the actor are often either most personal or rather dotty, and if they produce a result, they must be allowed. Exploration of himself should be an enjoyable process to the actor, but somehow it must interest him beyond his ego, and give him a sense of collective achievement; an emotional satisfaction that extends beyond the mere playing of his role.

The great school for the director is working with the actor in rehearsal: whatever ideas the director may bring as his offering, it is then that the actor invents a character, interpretation, emotion, attitudes, technical means, appearance and relationships. Whilst this invention takes place with the advice and encouragement of the director, the play must be shaped, in terms of narrative and action, climax and growth, sense and feeling. Ultimately the play must have a flow, a current between actors and audience, and the theatre is the only acting medium where the performer has any control of this power.

Apparent Meaning and Sub-text

The examination of the text during rehearsal should reveal what lies beneath the apparent surface meanings, and what motivations are behind the obvious intentions of characters. The secondary meanings and motives are the sub-text of the play. This sub-text may have much significance, or be a red herring. The scene from *The Way of the World* examined in an earlier chapter has most of its meaning fairly near the surface, and whilst the characters need to be motivated, to delve for psychological explanations would be as irrelevant as to ask what moving spirit guides Lady Bracknell, beyond what we can derive from what she says. She is a monstrous snob, with heavy-gunned wit, aristocratic disdain, a profound regard for propriety, and the conviction that God is a Tory. So we can deduce that Fainall is a villain, philanderer, charmer and cheat, Witwoud amusing, spiteful, affected yet friendly, and not very masculine. It would be pedantic to pursue the psychological possibilities that have made them so, to give emphasis and portentous inference that Fainall is a thwarted sadist with a deep sense of guilt, or that Witwoud was rejected by his family when a child. The sub-textual material here is the discovery of their world, its financial, social, and sexual reality, and what Congreve is saying about love and folly behind the elegant and amusing exchanges. Money is thrown away: the keeping up of appearance is more important than sincerity or integrity, friendship is a rare jewel, frivolity rules. A play which is very funny and apparently light-hearted on the surface turns out to be of serious intent, profound satire on a way of life that must be changed.

The naturalistic play, because of its limitations of form, generally contains more subtextual material: the dialogue of realism is a smaller dimension verbally, and says less than the poetic form, so much of the meaning is implied by tones of voice, attitudes, actions. So much is conveyed by the way a woman smokes a cigarette, stubbing it out half smoked, by a man's neglect of his clothes: by sighs, laughs, half-finished sentences. Sub-text is there to be discovered when the text does not make explicit statements. This is not to say that the formal text does not need the same careful sifting: the actor must satisfy himself that he understands the meanings of a complex structure of language, or he will substitute mere sound for sense: the hallmark of bad classical acting is shallow vocalizing.

From the establishment of sense and motive the actor moves towards inner meaning: even to a degree of identification with the character. It is impossible to say how much rehearsal should be devoted to the various aspects of performance: to moves, to interpretation, or characterization. Every play needs a different emphasis. The dramatic effect of the whole, and how it is conveyed, may be as different as Shaw and Beckett: from Shaw's logic, linear thinking and cause and effect to the non-events and metaphors and intuitions of Beckett. Shaw has often been attacked for using characters which are mere vehicles for his own ideas: the revolutionary and emancipated woman, the rational parasite, the reactionary moralist, and indeed there is a discernible tendency for one scintillating Shavian woman to sound rather like the next, for Undershaft and Mangan to have a similar line in sophistry. What emerges from rehearsal is that the dramatic life of his characters lies in powerfully articulated expression of attitudes. If Mrs Clandon did not take a violently prejudiced attitude to marriage, and endeavour to reduce human behaviour to a set of precepts, and if Fergus Crampton did not think that a woman's place was below the heel of her husband, the principal theme of marital responsibility and tolerance could not be explored in *You Never Can Tell.* Here we see that the actors must lend their personalities to the roles: Gloria Clandon is an exquisite creature, however stuffy and silly her progressive ideas may be.

Yet Vladimir and Estragon are not delineated as characters: the information about their age, appearance, speech, temperament, can only be inferred from the text:

ESTRAGON. Fancy that. (*He raises the remains of the carrot by the stub of leaf.*) Funny, the more you eat the worse it gets.
VLADIMIR. With me it's just the opposite.
EST. In other words?
VLAD. I get used to the muck as I go along.
EST. (*After prolonged reflection.*) Is that the opposite?
VLAD. Question of temperament.
EST. Of character.
VLAD. Nothing you can do about it.
EST. No use struggling.
VLAD. One is what one is.
EST. No use wriggling.
VLAD. The essential doesn't change.

A characteristic exchange: Vladimir the loftier, the gloomier, showing a sense of nicety in expression. Estragon more sentimental, less acute, relishing the platitude. A multitude of small inferences must be digested before their attitudes emerge clearly, and they must be endowed with a realism of speech and personality. Again, the actor here is going to draw on his own personality, and ask "If I were Estragon ...?"

Trust and the Unspoken Exchange

While rehearsing the director looks for signals from the actor. Often these are unconscious: a tone of voice, a gesture. Something tiny may be the germ of a performance: woe betide the director if he misses the moment when the first true intimation of the character appears. The play also sends out signals: just to speak the lines makes revelations. The rehearsal is a haphazard process of birth. All the logical methods of deduction and elimination must be used, then "It" must start to happen. "It" is something instinctive, something that feels right to actor and director. The response to the signal is a matter of feeling, seldom of logic: the actor must be encouraged to pursue the hunch. An appeal to intelligence often doesn't help: the emotions and imagination need stimulating. Michael Aldridge tells of a characterization that was triggered off by a costume: playing the thankless part of the wet Captain Vane in *The Magistrate* he found the character elusive: he's on the stage a lot, and says little to any effect. A visit to the costumiers produced a long cylindrical overcoat with a monstrous collar, like a costume by Erte, which fired his imagination with a character he could feel and understand: a precarious, teetering military dandy, lurking timidly in his huge coat, a mouse brandishing a sabre.

The director must trust an actor when the character is beginning to cohere, and when it isn't. Many good actors cannot deliver the goods early in rehearsal, indeed the actor who does is rather alarming: what more is there to come? Can the idea be maintained, while other actors are in a process of changing their ideas and methods? The good actor of some experience is a wary creature in early rehearsals: will read indifferently, and commit himself to the role with great hesitation. Rehearsal must be slowed down when an actor is achieving objectives too fast: he may be trying to impose a superficial performance on the production. A very elusive quality of a good rehearsal is the degree of exchange between actors: they should in general arrive at the same rough stage of development together. Often a series of separate, disconnected performances, however good individually, will fail to make a play work. The interchange between actors starts with listening acutely to each other: looking at each other, really understanding the interchange. An under-rehearsed production invariably gives the impression that actors are merely waiting for cues, or attempting to dominate or abdicate. Spontaneity depends on the ability to listen at every performance as if the dialogue had never been spoken before.

Rehearsal, then, falls into two areas: the process of helping the actor by a creative atmosphere, by advice and discussion, by helping him to relate his work to others, and the business of shaping the play as a whole. This may mean a lot of attention to the minutiae of acting and production: moves, speech, timing. The two jobs must move along harmoniously side by side, with attention to production appearing very much the secondary consideration: the actor rapidly loses confidence if he feels that his performance is only subordinate to the concept and effect of the whole production. To dictate to the actor purely to obtain an effect is a desperate measure, and shows that the actor hasn't been persuaded to see a particular dramatic possibility for himself. It is an old saw of directing that the director should plant an idea in the actor's head, wait for him to make use of it, then praise him for thinking of it. Funnily enough actors tend to say exactly the same of directors! Clearly there should be a mutual sympathy and joy at discovering the play together, and praise, whether entirely merited or not, is a most useful lubricant. Many fine directors and actors do not possess the ability to express an idea with total succinctness, but may make a useful point none the less.

Shape: Attack and Tempo

Timing and variation of pace to regulate the reception of ideas and feeling will probably not establish itself till a play is well rehearsed. Yet finally every moment, speech, move, will be polished to achieve a specific end, and every scene of the play given a tempo which relates it to the whole. We tend to think that certain plays have a specific quality of timing, and must ask whether it is true or false: for example the English concept of the comedies of Chekhov, laden with gloomy pauses inimical to comedy, or the violent pace sometimes given to farce. Only the text itself can reveal the tempo of a play: the criterion is how fast the thoughts and actions and utterances are to express a particular truth; a well-executed double-take says something very exact about thought and recognition. A "good house" for a comedy will add minutes to the playing time, not in the texture of the actor's performances, but in their strategy in handling the audience: passages of rapid dialogue become sporadic as they become interspersed with laughs. This variation in tempo, which cannot be rehearsed, means that the actor and director must get as much experience of audience as they can: technique is needed to handle an audience. "Attack," the conjunction of thought, speech, action and energy must be adjusted: the actor may have to lift the voice when picking up the line after a pro-tracted laugh, or underplay when he judges the audience to be in an attentive, acutely listening mood. A long speech, a very "talky" passage of dialogue, may need slight variations of pace and volume: the audience may be slumbering at a matinée and need speed and vigour to stimulate them, or be restless and fidgety, and need slightly more deliberateness of pace and timing. Always the actor must sense the audience: what can be built into the production in terms of timing is the point from which he departs in performance.

Final Rehearsals

The play reaches a point when the facts are known and the objectives firmly in sight. Reappraisals will not help the actor at this point, nor will detailed notes relating to character and relationship. The best help the director can give is to devote himself to practicalities of timing and clarity, efficiency of moves and business; also integration of the performances with the technical effects, stage management and lighting. It is most important to keep the actor calm, to remove from his path anything that may throw him. The challenge of arriving at performance is all he or she needs, but the theatre tends to thrive on false crises—"Act two must be rewritten by tomorrow morning!" In the last stages of rehearsal the director should look for cohesion, for further subtle stages of growth, and should exude confidence, which he may be very far from feeling. With luck the play will take off: actors start quite spontaneously to do things which invest their performances with humanity, detail, responsiveness: a clothing of the bones with living flesh, a quality which cannot be described or asked for; it is peculiar to the good, well-rehearsed actor in performance. Running through is the final stage that makes the play come to life as a whole, and there must be enough runs to make the actor secure, but not complacent: a sense of rising to a peak. To run through too often stales the actor and takes away some of the challenge and excitement, and a mood of doubt or indifference may set in. The director is an audience of one at this stage and his reaction must be very subtly judged: every actor after a run will be on tenterhooks to know how they have done. The more technical the play the more runs it will need, to give smoothness to entrances, exits, changes of mood and thought. A play with one set and a small cast clearly only needs running for the actors' sake, and is exhausting to the actors. The changes in performance at the late stages should be small and subtle. The actor who says "It'll be all right on the Night" and improvises, however brilliantly, is no actor: he is relying only on inspiration, which may not descend from heaven, and certainly will not descend on other members of the cast when given a wrong cue or move.

Dress rehearsal should proceed in several stages, according to the needs of the play. If there are numerous cues of a technical nature, involving entrances, exits, actors cueing technical effects, a "top-and-tail" session should precede the first dress run. At this stage, while each cue is checked with actors and technicians, dress and make-up can be approved and stage management problems and quick-change difficulties can be ironed out. Obviously, anything involving the actor must be rehearsed in full, for example a change of clothing must be practised exactly as it will be done in performance.

Following this comes the first stagger-through: an amalgamation of performance and technicians, drawing together all the elements of the production. It will probably be very untidy: the actor for the first time has to perform in the set: cues will be early and late, props and scenery will cause delays and difficulties. Such a rehearsal should only stop in the face of insurmountable crisis: the staff must somehow cope as if it were a performance, and the director should take notes of all technical problems, as opposed to acting difficulties: it is very unlikely that the actor will do anything but mark through the performance under such circumstances. After the first stagger-through, a trouble-shooting session, dispensing with the actors if possible; then on to dress rehearsal proper, in all conditions simulating a performance. Some plays, comedy for example, benefit from a final dress rehearsal before an invited audience, so that the actor may go into the first night with a little more idea of likely audience reaction. Dress rehearsal is a great imponderable: theatre tradition would have it that a shambles of a DR is a good omen, on the assumption that desperation will raise everybody to great feats. Better that DR should be efficient: the thought of imminent performance should be enough to create an atmosphere of excitement!

7
Technical Staff and Stage Management

We must now consider the functions and methods of the production staff in rehearsing and running the show. The technology of theatre has advanced so rapidly that skilled and fully trained operatives are needed in every department. Stage management is not a job for a frustrated actor, nor a recommendation for an acting job. Willingness, a thick skin, and the ability to make good tea and coffee are not enough. Most schools of drama run a training course for stage management students, not only to staff their own productions, but to supply the urgent needs of the profession. Such students are thus qualified to work in a junior capacity: after a few years of experience rising to the level of general stage manager, though to work well in this sort of position is not merely a matter of technical know-how, but of authority, personality, the capacity to manage people. Training for the stage management student embraces all aspects of technical theatre: running a show, handling scenery, rehearsal procedure, prop-making, the management of scenery, and sound and lighting operations. The role of the SM is a wide one, covering all the technical aspects of the production, and his support is essential to the director for the smooth and efficient progress of rehearsal and performance: indeed, when the show has opened it is in the charge of the stage and company manager: the director's authority by then is a matter of courtesy. The gathering together of a good stage management staff is a first consideration, and in the amateur theatre it may be necessary for the director to train his own technicians. For the purpose of this book it is necessary to simplify, since technical theatre deserves several books to itself.

At the top of the production staff we have the General stage manager, sometimes combining the duties of company and production manager. A GSM may work in a company, or a company with several activities, for example a repertoire theatre, and this is a job for an experienced SM with a considerable knowledge of technical theatre, and a lot of managerial capacity. To be more specific, his activities may take in the supervision and running of two shows, and other activities like a Theatre in Education or children's shows. A stage manager who has a lot of activities to oversee cannot run shows himself, but should be able to cope in an emergency. The capacity to deal with crises is a most important attribute, and there are a multitude of other duties: these could include liaison with design staff, the calling and scheduling of rehearsal, and the provision of all technical facilities from wigs to lighting equipment. Nobody has ever defined the job: it can be expected of such an SM that he or she is capable of a watching brief over almost any of the activities within a theatre. Other duties may include payment of artists' salaries, company morale and discipline, supervision of theatre catering, rehearsing understudies, arranging tours, organizing rehearsal facilities, and certainly overseeing the work of the stage technicians. In fact, just about everything except acting or directing! The production manager as such would have no stage management responsibilities but would be concerned exclusively with the output of scenic and prop workshops and wardrobe, and with the work of the technicians—clearly a job for a man or woman of parts, who has been thoroughly grounded in the subordinate jobs.

Staffing a Production

Each production should have attached to it a stage manager who knows the show both technically and artistically: it's his baby and he takes charge of the running of the show once it has opened. With him are two assistants, one to keep the "book" and document the production, and to prompt during rehearsals, the other to furnish props, rehearsal props, set-up for rehearsal, and during the running of the show to supervise all movement of scenery and properties. In practice, the SM will probably run the show, if it's at all difficult: many light, sound, and scenic cues need a cool head, and an experienced sense of timing. The immediate responsibility for the proper handling of the show is his, and he and his assistants should be prepared to turn their hands to anything in the interest of efficiency; many productions get on with no carpenter, no property master, and no stage-hands. It might appear that the lion's share of stage management is done by two ASMs, but this should not be so. The GSM should be present, helping his assistants to find the quickest, quietest, and simplest way of serving the production. Perfection is the only objective: the margin for error is nil. A flown piece of scenery may mar a scene by touching the stage one second late, or a sound cue too early may get the biggest laugh of the evening. Acting error is easier to hide than technical mistakes. Polished presentation needs scrupulous attention to detail.

The Book: The Key to Organized Rehearsal and Performance

Clear documentation is essential for smooth rehearsal. The ideas thrown up by director and actors are in a state of constant change, and there must be a means of checking exactly what was done at the last rehearsal, to clarify moves and positions: the stumbling actor, fishing for words and moves needs help when rehearsal has to be speedy. If the director is evolving movement in an improvisatory way, either throughout or in specific scenes, everything must be recorded, or it means virtually starting from scratch at the next rehearsal. Actors should, but often don't, write down the moves and business they are given, and it's common-sense and kind to help somebody with a big part needing a lot of concentration. The director simply must be able to get his eyes off the page and on to the actor as soon as rough blocking is done. Just as a good ASM notes the wilder paraphrases, and discreetly tells the actor at a break, so he or she notes down altered moves, and checks with the actor: the director will probably be think-ing of twenty others things, so won't have noticed. The approach should be "Do you want to change that move upstage?" and "Are you cutting the sit on that line?" rather than "You've got the moves ALL WRONG!" as if assuming that the actor is drunk or doddering. The ASM on the book needs to be a tactful but firm person and to keep even the director on the rails. The setting out of moves in the prompt copy must be done in pencil, and needs a kind of shorthand in the cause of speed, thus:

UR upstage right	UC upstage centre	UL upstage left
R stage right	C stage centre	L stage left
DR downstage right	DC downstage centre	DL downstage left

Further abbreviations are:

X cross (e.g. XDLC.) R rise: P or p long or short pause: indicate turns, and the actor's eyeline after the turn: arrows thus show the precise direction of a cross, longer arrows showing the track of a move, thus:

It is wise in the case of a scene using a number of actors, with much movement and changing of grouping, to draw a quick diagram of the group as it is at the top of each page of dialogue, using the initial letter of the name of the character, thus:

FIG 3 *Lear interrogating his daughters, showing any significant eye-lines, in this case Cordelia's. × marks the attendants.*

The script must be interleaved with a sheet of plain paper opposite every page of text, dialogue or stage directions, and the information on it set out in columns: moves, being most relevant to rehearsal, set next to the printed page and every move related to a specific moment in the text. This may be done by inserting a number in a circle, or by drawing a line connecting the move to the point in the text where it is initiated (see opposite).

Whatever method best suits the stage manager should be used, provided it can be quickly referred to.

The recording of moves should occupy a narrow column, say one-third of the page, the remainder of which is to accommodate in similar columns all technical details relevant to actually operat-

MASHA.	. . . Andrey, come here for a moment will you? Just for a moment, dear. (*Enter Andrey.*)	X to USR
OLGÀ.	This is my brother, Andrey Serghyeevich.	A & M x DL
VERSHININ.	Vershinin.	Bows
ANDREY.	Prozorov. (*Wipes the perspiration from his face.*) I believe you've been appointed battery commander here?	Bows I^A_V^M O x slowly R
OLGA.	What do you think, dear? Alexander Ignatyevich comes from Moscow.	I O A M V
AND.	Do you, really? Congratulations!	I x UR

Or the other method:

VERSH.	I'm afraid your sisters must be getting tired of me already. ①	① I to DS to R of V
IRENA.	Just look, Ander gave me this little picture frame today. (*Shows him the frame.*) He made it himself.	
VERSH.	Yes, it's . . . it's very nice indeed—	
IRENA.	Do you see that little frame over the piano? He made that one, too. ② (*Andrey waves his hand impatiently and walks off.*)	② A x URC
OLGA.	He's awfully clever, and he plays the violin ③ and he makes all sorts of things, too. In fact, he's very gifted all round. ④ Andrey, please don't go. ⑤ He's got such a bad habit, always going off like this. Come here!	③ M x UR ④ O C us, follow up ⑤ M turns A DS M A I V

ing the show, with a column each for lighting cues, scenic or flying movements, and sound cues, if there are many. If a production is technically simple it is merely necessary to enter each category of cue in a different-coloured pencil, to eliminate the possibility of confusion between types of cue. Each cue must further be numbered in its category, e.g. LXQ9, SFX4, and so on. Each technical operator needs warning before the carrying out of a cue, in general a page of dialogue in advance, but this is a matter of commonsense agreement: however, in the script the "warn" must be entered in the appropriate column, as WARN LXQ21, and connected to GO LXQ21 by a vertical line in coloured pencil, to draw the eye to the actual moment of operating. This needs to be noted in the text at a precise moment; also in the appropriate colour. Where an intercom system exists, actors will need to be warned when they are due on stage, a matter of judgement; where there is no intercom, and there is a lot of marshalling of actors, calls must be given in person by one of the stage management. Half, quarter, five minute and beginners calls should be done live, to ensure that the actors actually are present, not in the adjacent bar.

Let us compress a couple of pages of text to show technical documentation: this is not to suggest that flown scenery is *de rigueur* in *The Merchant of Venice*! (see opposite).

The only object of such a layout is to eliminate the possibility of mistakes. The prompt corner is a silent, but hectic place where split-second decisions must be made, including the "go" for perhaps several tons of scenery!

The prompt copy must also contain names, addresses, and phone numbers of cast and staff, and suppliers of facilities, outside contractors, etc.; whom to speak to at the costumiers, the furnishers, the sound suppliers, and so forth. The documentation of prop and scenery settings can be included in the prompt copy if few in number, but should also be separately listed: a complete copy for all stage management staff, and separate lists for the various technicians: props, carpenter, etc. Each scene change should be listed, in order starting from the off-prompt side of the stage, and including offstage props set on stand-by tables. Flats when used should be organized into packs, so that they travel the shortest possible distance to the point of setting: each flat, appropriately marked, e.g. PS 1, PS 2, etc., and stacked in order. Changes need scrupulous organization: props, starting with carpets and furniture, go on first in setting and go off last in striking. Action props have first priority, as opposed to dressing. Positioning of furniture and scenery should be finally

Enter Jessica, above.

Call
PORTIA, NERISSA,
MOROCCO, ATTENDANTS

JESSICA.   Who are you? Tell me, for more
certainty,
Albeit I'll swear that I do know
your tongue.

LORENZO.   Lorenzo, and thy love.

JESSICA.   Lorenzo, certain; and my love
indeed;
For who love I so much? And now
who knows
But you, Lorenzo, whether I am yours?

Warn SFX
Q9

LOR.   Heaven, and thy thoughts, are
witness that thou art.

Warn LX
Q15

JESS.   Here, catch this casket; it is
worth the pains.

Warn
FLIES
Q7

I am glad 'tis night, you do not
look on me,
For I am much ashamed of my exchange;
But love is blind, and lovers
cannot see
The pretty follies that themselves
commit,
For if they could, Cupid himself
would blush,
To see me thus transformed to a boy.
....

GRATIANO.   . . . . I desire no more delight
Than to be under sail, and gone tonight.

60 LX
Q15

Exeunt

Enter Portia, Nerissa, attendants.

60 FLIES
Q7

60 SFX Q9

PORTIA.   Go draw aside the curtains. . . .

established at lighting rehearsal, and marks made on the stage
with plastic tape, thus, indicating the knuckle or end of a flat:

⌐ knuckle;   ⌐ corner;   ⌐ end.

In a professional theatre, the responsibility for technical work
breaks down thus: each department has a chief, or head of
department: the carpenter is responsible for setting and striking

scenery and rostra, and the property master for all furnishings and props. All these technicians, including the chief electrician and head flyman, operate under the supervision of the stage management: naturally experienced technicians must be supervised tactfully.

The most important aspect of the management of scenery, lights, props and sound is the manner in which it is organized: usually the director doesn't think about it until he presides at a dress rehearsal where nothing works, where scenery is out of place and props missing. The proper training and degree of enthusiasm of the staff are vital to the success of a production: their meticulous attention to detail, flair, and spirit of co-operation with actors gives a production the quality of finish the public and actors are entitled to expect. Every director should develop and encourage a team, and foster their relations with the actors: the actor must feel secure and the technician appreciated.

Production Meetings

It is the stage manager's job to set up production meetings at appropriate times. These are essential periodic planning or trouble-shooting sessions, at which the director must make decisions, which directors don't like doing. The director is advised and informed in this process by any or all of the following: designer, production manager, GSM or DSM, costume designer/wardrobe, lighting designer/electrician, sound technician, composer, chief technician/carpenter, publicity manager. The first meeting is a discussion where the director sets out the practical and artistic needs of the production, and makes any compromises necessary to ensure that it's on time and within budget, and if he's wise, picks the brains of his co-artists and technicians. Scheduling of rehearsal, scenic and costume fitting deadlines are pencilled in, and proposed DR and production dates established. Halfway through rehearsal another meeting should take place. This is by way of a progress report, and the last chance for major modifications or changes of plan. Finally, there should be a last meeting pre dress rehearsal to arrange the very tight schedule for lighting, technical matters, wardrobe, set up and DR. ENOUGH TIME must be allowed for all these activities: a competent

SM will lead his glassy-eyed director by the hand through all these processes, and tell him or her what he should be doing and when, and a sensible director will be very grateful for his powers of organization.

8
Basic Stage Lighting

The purpose of this chapter is to consider the fundamental principles of stage lighting. Lighting is now a considerable side industry within the theatre, and in film and television studios, and has achieved a high level of sophistication, especially in the field of musical and operatic theatre. The elevation of the lighting man to lighting designer, and the appreciation of his artistic contribution, derives from two sources. First, film and television, where high-quality lighting, subtle visual images, and pictorial clarity are a prime necessity: secondly from the development of theatre as spectacle, with the Victorian actor-managers lighting dramatically and realistically with gas! The quantity and quality of equipment in use have changed radically in the last two decades, due in part to the lighting consultant, who is interested not only in good lighting but also in exchanging new lamps for old: two lamps and more are used instead of one: this is not merely Parkinson's law but public demand for visual presentation of a spectacular quality. As lighting is such a visual priority, however, it is preferable to have too much equipment rather than too little at one's disposal.

Intention and Purpose

The purpose of lighting is simple: to make the actors and the action visible: to create atmosphere, time and place: contrasts of mood, and emphasis of a dramatic kind. Lighting contributes most potently to the audience's emotions. First, however, the actor must be lit, wherever he is on stage, and from two opposite angles: there are seldom occasions when a source of light is exclusively one-directional. Even a man by a window in a dark room is receiving some reflected light on the side of his face away from the window. As each acting area is lit from opposed angles, with perhaps more emphasis on one side (the supposed source of light), the beams of light must merge before reaching the actor, or he is seen to be in two distinct, separate sources of light. The beams of any two or three lanterns lighting an acting area must merge at head height. Lighting of scenery is a secondary consideration to providing well-lit acting areas for the actor: however, if the actor is lit suitably for visibility and atmosphere, this same quality of light must also embrace the setting.

Equipment and Control

The director needs to know what lighting equipment is available, how and where it is to be used, and to what extent it can be controlled. First, control. Ideally, every circuit (carrying one or two lamps, preferably one) should have its own dimmer channel, thus enabling the operator to control the quantity of light most selectively, but this is expensive, and the number of dimmer channels is often reduced by the use of lighting circuits in "pairs," or by "patching" which allows the choice of circuits to be plugged into the number of dimmer channels available. A great variety of control systems are available, ranging from a simple dimmer board with eight circuits and four slider resistance dimmers, to the sophisticated computerized remote control of two or three hundred thyristor dimmers. The small control system of today uses thyristor dimmers, remotely controlled instead of manually operated resistance dimmers; the flexibility of such units is such that the standard module may vary in capacity from a six-channel, six-lever desk to an eighty-channel control with three pre-sets. The thyristor dimmer control may also embrace a "memory" system for pre-setting. If the power supply permits, the control system can be extended by hiring extra control equipment. The lighting equipment itself falls into two categories: floodlights and spotlights: the first distributing low-intensity light with a wide beam angle and useful for area lighting, that is atmospheric light of a particular colour quality, or for lighting large surfaces with a general wash of light, backings, cloths, cycloramas. The second type of lantern is the spotlight, throwing a controllable beam of high-intensity light. This directed beam can be controlled in its beam angle, and may be either hard-edged ("profile"), lighting only a specifically defined area, or soft-edged, whereby the beam can be easily merged with other directed light. The profile spot, generally from 500W to 2 kW, is mainly for use in front-of-house positions, or for a long throw to the stage: the clear edge of its beam ensures a freedom from "spill" on to the audience below, or on to the surrounds of the stage, proscenium, border, etc. To this end, shuttered lanterns are probably most useful in the FOH, so that the beam may be shaped at either side, top and bottom, giving a horizontal, vertical, or angled cut-off. FOH lighting must have adequate power to balance the light behind the prosc., or actors moving below the prosc. can be seen to enter a dimmer area as they move downstage. The bi-focal spot gives a choice of hard or soft edges, and clearly has an FOH application when lighting the downstage area. The profile spot also has a usefulness above the acting area itself: to deliver light in a precise shape, for example framing up a door or a window, or covering an exact area in size. The soft-edged spot, with "Fresnel" lens, gives a diffuse-edged beam, of variable angle, easily intermixed, and is of most use cross-lighting the acting area at a shorter distance: the beam when striking scenery or objects presents a pool of light with gradually fading edges, not the clear outline of the profile spot. The Fresnel lens spot can be regarded as a high-intensity flood of great variability: its beam may be further controlled by the use of "barn doors," external four-sided shutters. Floods are necessary for washing light over large flat surfaces: backings, cloths, etc.: it is important that they are not placed too close to the surface they are lighting or hot spots will result. They may be flown, vertically mounted, or stood on the stage floor. Footlights, or "floats" are in little use in the theatre of today, their cardinal principle being to provide a small amount of light from below, thereby avoiding deep shadowing from overhead lighting: they are traditionally beloved of leading ladies (and leading men) because of their ability to remove double chins and bags under the eyes. The greater efficiency and power of stage lighting usually ensures enough bounce back from the stage surface to render them unnecessary. Certainly they provide a quality of warmth and intimacy, and are in great demand for kitchen scenes in Panto, but used to excess they look as if Hell is yawning and the floor on fire. A general layout for the proscenium theatre would be: the DS area covered by FOH, the area upstage from the proscenium covered by the No. 1 and No. 2 spot bars:

combinations of lamps from these three sources may be necessary to cover all the acting areas. When a large setting must have a general quality of illumination, for example the big, glittering set-piece scenes of musicals, it may be necessary to add flood lighting above the acting area, directed vertically downward, providing atmospheric lighting of a particular nature. On the small stage it has long been the practice to use a compartment batten, or magazine, for overall general illumination. These are merely small floods in a continuous casing, usually arranged to produce three-colour circuits, and greatly in favour for lighting the unsuitable stage: generally containing fly-blown filters of deep amber, primary red, and deep blue, which successfully stop most of the light reaching the actors beneath. The advantage of the individual flood is flexibility: it may be directed and controlled by swivelling or hooding. The perch position, roughly between floor and No. 1 bar, sometimes a swing arm mounting, is useful for giving close spotlighting on the downstage extremities. Boom lighting is any equipment carried vertically on either side of the stage, in effect from the wings, to produce directional sidelighting, and must be used with discretion. Other equipment may stand freely—floods for general illumination of offstage but visible areas, spots for specific effects (e.g. light through windows on actors' faces), and effects projectors, high-intensity lanterns throwing pictorial images on to screens or backings. The latter must be allowed space for proper enlargement of the image: the ideal place for the projector is behind the scenery, allowing the actor to move in front of it.

Using Colours

Before considering the basic design of lighting, we must think of the use of colour filters. Colour will enhance the picture but reduce the amount of light the lanterns will deliver, so if there are too few the lighting must use white light wherever possible. Colour is often garishly overused, particularly in the amateur theatre. A wide range of colour filters is available, from primary colours to delicate tints. The most frequently used are the gold tints and pale pinks, Strand Cinemoid Nos. 51–54, for their warm effect on the human face; No. 36, surprise pink (lavender), a useful pink-blue combination; 1, 2, 3, the pale yellow-straw range; 17 and 40, steel blue and light blue; 29 and 31, light and heavy frost, which simply diffuse and soften white light; and chocolate tint, pale chocolate, and grey, 55, 56, and 60, which take the harsh edge off white light. Coloured light has a specific effect on coloured objects: white light, containing all the colours of the spectrum, reflects the colour of the objects it falls on, while absorbing the others: coloured light enhances its own colour, so a scene may be made warm or chilly by lighting it with pink/gold or blue. Certain combinations of colour produce a black object: blue light on a yellow costume will make it appear nearly black. It is apparent that the stronger filters are used to best effect when they must create a striking quality of light, for example firelight; or when importing their colour to a light surface, for example to produce sunset on a cyclorama.

Bear in mind that colours need to be mixed: a scene may require a warm atmosphere, and be lit with 52 pale gold, and another scene in a different acting area be largely lit with lavender and steel tint. The two areas may not be homogeneous when lit simultaneously: the change in the lighting will be apparent and must have a justification—one part of the area receives direct light, the other is in shadow. As a general rule, the warm light is from a light source, the colder from shadow. The choice of colour for the production must stem from the colour of costume and scenery: whether it is to be enhanced, as one might enrich with lighting the colours of a sunlit scene, or whether a quality of mood predominates, when all the colours of setting and costume are subordinate to a sullen sky.

Planning: Coverage and Effect

At an early stage of planning, director and lighting designer must discuss the proposed treatment of each scene, and any effects needed: the sources of light for the scene: windows, artificial lighting, natural lighting, moonlight—both direction, and the mood to be created. The lighting designer or electrician at this stage must supply a layout of equipment: how the lamps are rigged, what part of the stage each lamp can cover, the possibilities of controlling the lighting. From this discussion emerges what parts of the stage are strongly lit: it is pointless to light areas that are little used, or difficult to light, for example next to the scenery: what sort of colours may be used, with consideration of the contrast from scene to scene; sheer shortage of lamps may limit the possibilities of obtaining dramatic change from a scene of brilliant moonlight to a scene of sunlight. The lighting designer must produce for the director a plan, showing which lamp is lighting which part of the stage, and how it is coloured: this should be before moves are finally settled, so that the acting areas are making the best use of the available equipment. Problems must be planned for, the use of special effects, the use of cyclorama; if actors are moving close to a skycloth, shadows must be eliminated by the provision of extra sidelighting upstage. Any projected effects, for example, the use of clouds on a cyclorama, which is more realistic than merely the use of colour, must allow for the throw of the projector. A simple projector can be created by adding a lens to a pattern 23 profile spot, and using mica or glass slides painted with Photopak. Moving effects are very powerful and will totally distract attention from the actor: if they are an essential, they may be used; if not, as an atmospheric gesture they are pretentious. The sky cloth, or backcloth may be lit on the small stage by compartment battens above and below: a larger cloth needs flooding all round, from a reasonable distance to avoid hot spots.

The preliminary lighting plot indicates how each scene is lit, and what lighting is covering the important acting areas. This will appear as a series of overlapping lit areas, showing the coverage of each lantern, and their respective colours: to most directors an academic matter till they see it in practice.

Lighting Rehearsal

The lighting rehearsal transforms theory into reality, and should be conducted with the actors or the stage management standing in for them: a set may look right, yet the lighting may be unsatisfactory for the actor moving about the stage. The start of lighting rehearsal must be to check that each lantern is covering the area specified on the lighting plan: since that time, moves will have extended and changed; an actor may be moving two feet further up stage, and consequently out of the area of the light; scenery may look slightly different under the effect of colour, and need a change of filter: changes must be made at this stage, before proceeding from cue to cue. Each lantern should be checked singly, in a black-out. Then follows a consideration of each lighting set-up, and the means of getting from cue to cue: timing, whether certain parts of the stage fade or light up before others, etc. The timing of cues is particularly important: a brief black-out may involve striking props, or the exit of several actors; a delayed cross fade may mean that actors enter speaking in relative darkness. Whilst the operator must be encouraged to use his initiative, he can only operate when given cues: if he is to take cues from a visual action on the stage, he must be able to see all of it. The lighting operator needs rehearsal with a complex series of cues, and each one should be rehearsed, in conjunction with stage management, until perfectly timed. In a production with complex lighting, needing the co-operation of the actors, they must rehearse at some time each cue with which they are involved, and make the necessary adjustments of position to be properly lit: when working in a small area of light a distance of six inches can take the actor's face out of the light. If the actors are not so rehearsed, but are aware that they must be lit, they can be seen to be "finding their light," to the discomfort of the audience. It is vital that in lighting rehearsals the director knows the number and purpose of each lamp, so that when asking the operator for changes, he can specify it by numbers, rather than vaguely saying "It's a bit dark upstage left of the sofa."

The aim of the director should be a proper balance of light: as moves direct the audience where to look, so must lighting. The first need is the "key" lighting, that is the principal acting areas. Next, the secondary lighting: areas less used, less brightly lit; finally the "fill-in" lighting: offstage areas which are visible, outside doorways, windows, etc. Every realistic source of light, be it a window or a table-lamp, needs augmentation: a flat, bright or dim wash of light over set and actors destroys the appearance of a production. The open stage presents an extra problem. A thrust stage must clearly be lit from three angles most of the time, and the in-the-round area from 360 degrees. Whilst the same principles of multi-directional lighting and realistic and enhancing colour and intensity apply, some of the lighting is opposite the audience; consequently it must be rigged as high as possible, to avoid shining in their eyes. Much use must be made of bifocal and profile spots when they are hung above the heads of the audience, to avoid both spill and illumination of the front rows.

During recent years, it has become less necessary to hide the machinery of the theatre from the audience, and in the case of lighting equipment this is sometimes impossible, particularly on an open stage, where there can be no provision for borders to mask the equipment. The aim of lighting should be to do its job unobtrusively, not to draw the eye up to the equipment itself, and accessibility and flexibility is a must: during a lighting rehearsal from twenty to two hundred lamps may need adjustment.

Lighting is both a basic necessity, and a final enhancement to a play—a supplement to the work of the director and designer, who can learn much about the use of light from the work of artists throughout the centuries, and by developing their visual sense to the full. Visibility at all times is the priority, followed by the creation of mood and atmosphere: *The Cherry Orchard* would lose much of its subtlety of place and feeling without a true creation of shadows in empty rooms, the sad tranquillity of a sunset.

9
Style, Convention and Interpretation

The large consideration of style and convention needs careful understanding, because these qualities are indivisible from interpretation. Style is a vague term, which can mean élan, chic, opulence, and all too often means mere sophistication. It is also used as a set of convenient pigeon-holes to fit plays into—tragedy, comedy, farce, naturalism, classicism, etc. It suggests that every play has an intrinsic quality, an identifiable structure and texture, and that handled according to the rules it's likely to produce a certain type of response. This is to confuse style with convention, which would appear to be a recognizability of mode, content and character, with which the audience is familiar, from genre to ritual. A convention presumes an understanding, an attitude held by the audience. Style is a more detailed matter, and more elusive: perhaps homogeneity, certainly a subtle appositeness, a rightness of playing. Consider Feydeau's *A Flea in Her Ear*. This French farce belongs to a tradition of comedy and the sort of events likely to happen can be guessed at: perilous coincidences, mistaken identities, preposterous characters, a fast and wild farrago of action. Yet to play it in a vigorous, broad, yet exact manner does not endow it with style. The style emerges from something deeper: the values and passions of its characters, their attitude to love, romance, lust, fashion, respectability, honour, chivalry, and their own image of themselves. Style here may be taken to mean the *modus vivendi* of the characters in conflict with their desires, their precise way of trying to have their cake and eat it, to assert their respectability and morality whilst enjoying a little slap and tickle on the side. So gentility and the more comical aspect of passion appear to be essential ingredients, conditioning behaviour. In contrast, *Look Back in Anger* is a play in the convention of social realism, in almost every aspect naturalistic. The minutiae of detail in acting and production are vitally important, the squalor of a miserable little flat, clothes worn too long and too often, and the characters' utterly realistic encounter with their lives and each other. It must not be turned into a didactic metaphor, where Jimmy and Alison merely represent attitudes to life: its style is in the pangs of recognition, absolute verisimilitude.

Falsity of Style

A misunderstood concept of style may cause actors to strive for an apparent predominant effect, at the expense of truth. For example, for many years the comedies of the Restoration were seen as displays of wit and elegance above all, with little attention given to the realistic elements of the characters' world. This is to take attention away from the central themes; satire and mockery of greed and ambition, passion, frivolity and vanity, set in a world of fine clothes with a dirty rump underneath. Mincing and fan-waving, red heels and periwigs should not turn into fancy dress for suburban masters of badinage. Shakespeare and the Elizabethans have long been subjected to a false concept, which reflected a Victorian idea of virtue, evil, heroism and history, fine declamation, romantic women, a pseudo-heroic and virile manner of speech; the notable work of Peter Hall, Peter Brook, and John Barton during the last decade has done wonders to redress the balance, Naturally, the swing of the pendulum has produced some excesses, with today's hero in dark glasses and trendy clothes. Superficial adornment is not style, but stylishness. Style must be thought of as artistic reality, the means of expressing truth of character, meaning, mood—a simple definition of a quality that is infinitely difficult to achieve!

Style, Reality and Truth

Surely in our search for artistic reality we must relate to our own age, and that of the play. Historical acting methods reflect what people wanted from the theatre, regardless of the import of the play itself, and may be moribund. Our mode of handling classical drama is more idiomatic, more colloquial in its use of intonation and inflection, discarding booming, rhetoric, and over-rhythmic patterning of speech. Bernard Miles has experimented with Elizabethan acting methods, including the pronunciation of the sixteenth century, proving simply that the matter was merely of academic interest. Yet Ibsen or Chekhov, so much closer to us, seem to benefit from scrupulous fidelity to period: nineteenth-century Christian morality and attitudes, as expressed in Pastor Manders's language and conduct, are as essential as his basic psychology. We cannot play the man while throwing aside his mental clothes, nor present *Ghosts* in an utterly abstract setting. The furniture, the architecture is the spirit of the play: values asserted by covering up the legs of the piano.

Dramatists are not always bound by the matter of style, though they have usually tried to observe the conventions. It is the right of the artist to experiment, to mix, to use the method best suited to the expression of a particular idea, and tragedy and comedy, elegance and vulgarity are often found keeping company. Form is secondary to content, and variety and life are more interesting than correctness: consider the effect on an English audience of Racine in the manner of the Comédie Française: only the French can enjoy its subtle intimations. Periodicity is not merely the polite manners of an age, or its aesthetics, but the customs and philosophy of that age, and the stylistic balance must be inferred from the text: quite simply, how much does the external reality matter to the play?

Interpretation of Comedy: The Mixture of Modes

Let us examine a comedy from the interpretative point of view, to consider how the spirit of the play might emerge. Goldsmith's *She Stoops to Conquer* is a charming comedy, ostensibly belonging to the school of comedy of manners, but containing episodes of low comedy, near farce: Mrs Hardcastle entering from a dip in the horse-pond, as Tony Lumpkin gleefully announces, "draggled up to the waist like a mermaid" and having suffered every possible mortification:

> ... drenched in the mud, overturned in a ditch, stuck fast in a slough, jolted to a jelly, and at last to lose our way. Whereabouts do you think we are, Tony?

> By my guess, we should be on Crackskull Common, about forty miles from home.

> O Lud! O Lud! The most notorious spot in all the country. We only want a robbery to make a complete night on't.

Don't be afraid, Mamma, don't be afraid. (*Pause.*) Two of
the five that kept here are hanged, (*Pause.*) and the other three
may not find us. . . . Don't be afraid. IS THAT A MAN
THAT'S GALLOPING BEHIND US? (*In a small voice.*)
No, it's only a tree. . . .

I have added some stage directions here to indicate the way the
lines might be spoken for comic meaning. If farce can be thought
of as real characters in unreal situations, coping with preposterous
disasters, this is very like farce, especially for Mrs Hardcastle.
They are in the Hardcastles' garden. Tony has taken the coach
on a round trip, indulging in his ghoulish sense of humour:

. . . down Featherbed Lane, where we stuck fast in the mud.
I then rattled them crack over the stones of Up-and-Down
Hill. I then introduced them to the gibbet on Heavy-Tree
Heath, and from that, with a circumbendibus, I fairly lodged
them in the horse pond at the bottom of the garden.

The plot develops. Mr Hardcastle emerges for his nightly
constitutional:

AH! it's a highwayman with pistols as long as my arm! A
damned ill-looking fellow.

Hardcastle has heard them talking. Tony must get rid of him,
before Mrs Hardcastle discovers her whereabouts, so he engages
Hardcastle in an absurd conversation, putting on a foggy voice:

But I heard a voice here; I should be glad to know from
whence it came.

It was I, sir, talking to myself, sir. I was saying that forty
miles in three hours was very good going. HEM! As to be
sure it was. HEM! (*Pause.*) I have got a sort of cold by being
out in the air. We'll go in, if you please. HEM!

Tony's speech is dependent on good timing for its comic effect;
the timing shows his change of thought. The speech starts
bravely, for a man with a frog in his throat, but runs rapidly out
of steam as dawning incredulity shows in Hardcastle's face. . . .
"HEM! as to be sure it was. (*Small pause: he looks at Hard-*

castle, then low and rapidly.) **I have gotasortofcoldbybeingout-intheairwe'llgoinifyouplease** (*Grabbing him by the arm.*) **HERR-RMM!**" The comedy is compounded by the sudden asides of Mrs Hardcastle as she looms forth from behind the tree: "Ah Death! I find there's *danger.*" Her comic quality is passion.

Where does situation comedy end, and farce begin? We have in this play an intermixture of comic styles: comedy of character and situation, satire and wit. Consider the combinations of opposites in Marlow, scholar and libertine, man and mouse; an object of humour, but given to a lot of sharp satirical observation in his own right—earlier in the play we find him disposing of Hardcastle, whom he takes for a presumptuous innkeeper:

HARDCASTLE.	Here's a cup, sir.
MARLOW.	(*Aside, to Hastings.*) So, this fellow, in his Liberty Hall, will only let us have just what HE pleases.
HARD.	(*Taking the cup.*) I hope you'll find it to your mind. I have prepared it with my own hands, and I believe you'll own the ingredients are tolerable. Will you be so good as to pledge me, sir? Here, Mr Marlow, here is to our better acquaintance. (*He drinks, sits, and gives the cup to Marlow.*)
MAR.	(*Aside.*) A very impudent fellow this: but he's a character, and I'll humour him a little. (*To Hardcastle.*) Sir, my service to you.

Marlow, however, is cast in the role of victim, like a hero in Feydeau or Labiche, and has an absurd weakness:

> Happy man! You have talents and art enough to captivate any woman. I'm doomed to adore the sex, and yet to converse with the only part of it I despise. This stammer in my address, and this awkward, unprepossessing visage of mine, can never permit me to soar above the reach of a milliner's prentice or one of the Duchesses of Drury Lane. . . .

The opportunity for situation comedy cries out to be used, as indeed it is. What better than to put Marlow, stammer and all, in confrontation with the droll and delicious Kate Hardcastle? Though we warm to Marlow, the pleasure of seeing his pomposity debunked is irresistible: his failing is one of character, and doesn't engage our sympathy, and when he should bend he becomes starchy, when he should seek to please he seeks only to impress. His view of women, at both ends of the social scale, is naïve and sentimental:

> An impudent fellow may counterfeit modesty, but I'll be hanged if a modest man can ever counterfeit impudence. . . .

and:

> Why, George, I can't say fine things to them—they freeze, they petrify me. They may talk of a comet, or a burning mountain, or some such bagatelle: but to me, a modest woman, drest out in her finery, is the most **TREMENDOUS** object of the whole creation.

Exaggeration is a basic comedic device, and Marlow's estimation of women, and himself, especially his inability to talk to women of quality, is exaggerated. Here we get one pointer toward the style of the comedy: as style might be said to be the mode of life and thought of an age or society, Marlow's style may be said to be that of a man of sentiment, and inside the solemn humbug is a man of true and honest feeling, fighting to get out. Just as Marlow is foolish, according to intellectual fashion, so Kate is sensible, without losing one whit of her charm:

HARDCASTLE. . . . .The young gentleman has been bred a scholar, and is designed for an employment in the service of his country. I am told he's a man of excellent understanding.
KATE. Is he?
HARD. Very generous.
KATE. I *believe*. . . I shall like him.
HARD. And very handsome.
KATE. My dear papa, say no more (*She kisses his hand.*); he's mine. I'll have him.
HARD. And to crown all, Kate, he's one of the most bashful and reserved young fellows in the world.
KATE. Eh! You have frozen me to death again. That word reserved has undone all the rest of his accomplish-

HARD.

ments. A reserved lover, it is always said, makes a suspicious husband.

On the contrary, modesty seldom resides in a breast that is not enriched with nobler virtues. It was the very feature in his character that first struck me.

KATE.

He must have more striking features to catch me, I promise you. However, if he be so young, so handsome, so everything as you mention, I believe he'll do still. . . . I *think* I'll have him.

Hardcastle shows the same vein of sententiousness as Marlow, Kate a nice sense of irony. The actors playing Kate and Marlow need two obvious qualities, a polished external technique, and charm. The latter is such a subjective quality that it is impossible to define: certainly it's more than mere obvious good looks, perhaps youth, innocence, vitality, and vulnerability: without the latter Kate becomes a scheming creature: she makes the effort to reform Marlow not out of caprice, but out of sincerity.

Let us examine the scene of their encounter, with Kate meeting Marlow for the first time as herself: their previous meeting has been with Kate in the guise of poor relation, Marlow in his *alter ego* of seducer of the servants. The object of this examination is to try and divine how and why it is such a delightful comic scene. Hastings and Constance have left Marlow to Kate's tender mercy, to sink or swim. The scene starts with a bit of business: Marlow hovers, fetches a chair and sits down, there is a momentary pause, Kate looks at him: he has assumed a posture of ridiculous phoney nonchalance. Her indulgent smile reminds him that he has forgotten to draw up a chair for her: he leaps to his feet, she sits in his chair, he fetches another, and sits. His tempo has been broken, and he tries to start where he left off: he has sat half on, half off the chair. There is a pause; advantage, Kate.

KATE.

But you have not been wholly an observer, I presume, sir. The ladies, I should hope, have employed some part of your addresses. (*She draws her chair towards him.*)

MARLOW.

(*Relapsing into timidity.*) Pardon me, madam. I—I—I— as yet have studied-only-to-deserve them.

KATE.

And that, some say, is the very worst way to obtain them.

MAR.   Perhaps so, madam; for I love to converse only with
            the more grave and sensible part of the sex. (*He rises.*)
            But I'm afraid I grow tiresome.
KATE.   (*Quickly.*) Not at all, sir! (*Pause.*)

Here the timing is crucial. If Marlow rises hastily at the end of
the line "but I'm afraid I grow tiresome" and makes to turn
away; Kate thwarts the move by putting a restraining hand on
his arm, with the line "**NOT AT ALL,** sir!"; it's his expression
of agonized embarrassment that will produce the laugh. She
smiles, he winces, then she follows up:

KATE.   . . . . There is nothing I like *so much* as a grave con-
            versation myself; I could hear it forever. . . (*Hastily.*)
            indeed, I have often been surprised how a man of
            sentiment could ever admire those light, airy pleasures,
            where nothing reaches the heart.

It would appear that there is a laugh to be got after Kate's "I
could hear it forever." Her manner of speaking shares a meaning
with the audience that Marlow is far too distraught to catch.

MAR.   (*Sitting, moving his chair slyly away from her.*) It's
            a . . . disease—of the *mind*, madam. In the variety of
            tastes, there must be some who, . . . wanting a relish—
            for—um—a—um. . . .
KATE.   (*Cutting in rapidly.*) I understand you, sir. . . .

Here Kate scoops up the laugh by her cutting in at exactly the
right moment; Marlow is having trouble with the stammer, and
a conspicuous absence of anything sensible or amusing to say.
When words fail him, as they often do, he resorts to gestures,
wildly sawing the air to indicate his meaning: this sustains his
desperate energy, that of the drowning man. Kate must "top"
him, with an absolutely precise attack. She continues:

KATE.   . . . . there must be some, who, . . . wanting a taste for
            refined pleasures, pretend to despise what they are in-
            capable of tasting. (*She moves her chair toward him.*)

If Kate moves her chair neatly, quickly and deliberately, with a beady, sweet smile, she means business: words, vague slop, and action, have opposed meanings, and a laugh could be got on this piece of business, but its probably better to get on Marlow's follow-up:

MAR.   My meaning, madam, but infinitely better expressed.

Here he moves his chair in exactly the same manner as Kate: both do the action without changing their eye-lines or looking at the chair. The comic sub-text, of undignified pursuit, the chaser and the chased, is beginning to loom up amid all the high-sounding chat.

MAR.   . . . And I can't help observing that in this age of hypoc-
         risy, a—a—a——
KATE.   (*Aside, rapidly and desperately.*) Who could ever suppose
         this fellow impudent on some occasions! (*To him.*) You
         were going to observe, sir. . . .
MAR.   I was observing, madam—I protest, madam, I forgot
         what I was going to observe.
KATE.   (*Aside.*) I vow, and so do I.

This would seem to be a better place to get the laugh than on the aside four lines earlier, though a good actress would get both! However, there is a comic rhythm to this scene which should be felt for: too much clowning from Marlow undoes the dialogue, though it may get laughs. If necessary, the actors must pick up tempo to stifle premature laughs, and a short sequence leading to a laugh must be built in tempo to get to the point. At this point in the scene Kate's mood changes, from the hope that Marlow will say anything of a suitably wooing nature: she has found that the cure for Marlow must involve a change of strategy, and the rest of the interview is an exchange of vague moral truisms:

KATE.   . . . . You were observing, sir, that in this age of hypoc-
         risy—something about hypocrisy, sir. . . .
MAR.   (*Plunging on, desperately.*) Yes, madam; in this age of
         hypocrisy, there are few who upon strict enquiry, do not
         a—a——

KATE.   (*Swiftly.*) I understand you perfectly, sir——
MAR.   (*Aside.*) Egad! And that's more than I do myself.

Here Marlow gets a laugh by topping a sequence of lines: the effectiveness of his line is in its emotion: for the first time he's speaking the truth. Kate continues, with false brightness:

KATE.   You mean that in this hypocritical age, there are few
             who do not condemn in public what they practise in
             private, and think they pay every debt to virtue when
             they praise it?
MAR.   **TRUE, MADAM!!**

Kate rather wickedly summarizes the sort of thing Marlow has been spouting for several minutes: if Marlow's "True, Madam," bursts out we have built an amusing gag. Taking the initiative, and putting words into the mouth of a stammerer is like throwing a second custard pie at the man who's just wiped off the first one. On top of this little sequence, there is the possibility of a follow-up: Marlow bounces once more on the springboard before falling into the deep end.

MAR.   . . . . Those who have most virtue in their mouths, have
             least of it in their bosoms. (*He rises: very hastily*.) But
             I see Miss Neville expecting us in the next room. I
             would not intrude for the world.

Marlow throughout has been incapable of looking Kate in the eye: he is so carried away by his final indelicate utterance, that he actually looks at her, and leaps up in horror, upsetting the chair as he does so.

This is merely one set of possibilities that exist in the scene. The actors must play perfectly together, in terms of timing: they must possess the quality of sincerity that lies beneath the surface of the scene: and they must have a subtle control of the vocal line, Kate because she's indulging in a style of conversation not very congenial to her, Marlow because he stammers. His affliction is in the same cheerfully callous tradition as the banana-skin joke: very close to tragedy, very close to farce. Consider Martin in *Hotel Paradiso*, who kicks wildly every time he stammers, or Camille in

A Flea in Her Ear, who suffers from the misfortune of no roof to his mouth. The style of this play might be said to emanate from Goldsmith's attitude to his characters: the satire is genial and honest, an attack on false feeling, false sentiment, false manners. Even the lowly peasantry are affected by it, as this tiny snatch of dialogue reveals. Tony Lumpkin, that scourge of the fanciful, is entertaining his friends, a doubtful crew of horse-breakers, excisemen, etc. He has regaled them with a song, which declares booze to be the superior of religion or learning:

SECOND FELLOW. I loves to hear him sing, bekays he never gives us anything that's low.

THIRD F. Damn anything that's low; I cannot bear it.

FOURTH F. The genteel thing is the genteel thing at any time, if so be that a gentleman bees in a concatenation accordingly.

The Hardcastles themselves are made the subject of mockery, but with deep affection, not cruelty:

MRS HARDCASTLE. I vow, Mr Hardcastle, you're very particular. Is there not a creature in the country but ourselves does not take a trip to town now and then to rub off the rust a little? There's the two Miss Hoggs, and our neighbour, Mrs Grigsby, go to take a month's polishing every winter.

HARD. Ay, and bring vanity and affection to last them the whole year. I wonder why London cannot keep its own fools at home.

Tony puts sentimental attitudes in a nutshell:

Let her cry. It's the comfort of her heart. I have seen her and her sister cry over a book for an hour together, and they said they liked the book the better the more it made them cry.

Hardcastle himself has a somewhat different folly, but still a sentimental one: the conviction that things were better in the old days, and Mrs Hardcastle, sorely tried, says:

> Ay, your times were fine times indeed; you have been telling
> us of them for many a long year . . .

He is also a snob military, and a name-dropper

> Your talking of a retreat, Mr Marlow, puts me in mind of the
> Duke of Marlborough, when he went to besiege Denain. . . .
> "*Now*," says the Duke, to George Brooks, that stood next to
> him—you must have heard of George Brooks— "*I'll pawn
> my dukedom*," says he, "*but I take that garrison without
> spilling a drop of blood.*"

However, there is a delightful enthusiasm to Hardcastle, an innocent perplexity at the misunderstandings he creates. He and his
wife are developed as comic characters in considerable depth,
and their qualities as country gentlefolks are presented realistically, sympathetically: unlike the gross figures of Congreve and
Vanbrugh, Sir Wilful Witwoud and Sir Tunbelly Clumsy. The
style of playing must be rich in realism; Hardcastle might affect
a hearty and countrified mode of speech, pronouncing Marl-
borough as "*Mullllburrrugh.*" His wife, who longs to be above
all a woman of fashion, bedizens her appearance, and probably
bedizens her speech. She approaches badinage and social intercourse with elephantine delicacy: "Pray how do you like this
head, Mr Hastin's?" presenting her latest monstrous coiffure to
the suave Hastings, who of course is not lost for a flattering reply.
If her utterance lets her down and gives the lie to her pretensions,
she is comic, but wholly human and forgivable, to be gently
mocked yet relished: it is vital to capture her temperament, her
excitable girlishness, her mode of speech:

> Well, I vow, Mr Hastin's, you are very entertainin'. There's
> nothin' in the Warrld I love to talk of so much as Londerrn
> and the fasherrns, tho' I was never there meself!

We can see from these examples that style in this play springs from
interpretation and is an innate aspect of the characters, a mixture
of robust realism and absurd attitudes, coarseness and honest
feeling. The play mixes its comic modes vigorously, with the
eclectic freedom permitted to masterpieces: satire and criticism,

mockery and ridicule, yet achieved in a framework which reveals a love of human life (no misanthropist could describe such a dinner as that offered to Marlow and Hastings by Mr Hardcastle). Comedy of character, comedy of situation, wit, absurdity, and farce are all intrinsic in the play: the style is the balance of these qualities, the delicacy and deep humanity of its performance.

Attitudes to the Serious Drama

Style in the more serious drama is more difficult to define. Most comedy demands a lightness, a delicacy of touch, a technical expertness that flickers over a number of points, illuminates them brightly and passes on. Serious drama cannot be played on expertise alone, any more than it can be conveyed purely through deeply felt emotion. "Tragedy" presents a number of problems, including orotundity of speech, rhetoric without truth, self-indulgence and ponderous solemnity, and most adverse criticism seems to boil down to boredom and non-involvement, the very opposite of Aristotle's intellectual and moral purgation. The flaws in human psychology, the imperfections and tragic consequences of creeds and ethics are the aspect of tragedy that interest a modern audience. Contemporary thought would seem to steer us towards heroes both stoic and rational. Because we can conceive the protagonists of tragedy in terms of psychology, and thereby understand them better, we have lost some of their mystery, and the actor walks a narrow dividing line between pity and mirth, horror and mere revulsion. Can poetic speech be as "real" as prose? In itself, it may have a depth and lucidity in describing human experience, which naturalistic prose lacks. Bad naturalism trades only in the superficial and the trivial, being concerned with apparent lifelikeness, the general appearance of reality. Poetic language is not necessarily of metrical form, but rather more of heightened imagery, or meanings conveyed with a style that stimulates the imagination: it would seem to be a form of language that strives to be precise, rather than obscure or merely factual, and therefore needs less adornment than prose. A simple, limpid style of speech will allow an elaborately wrought text to do its work, and an honest, uncluttered style of production will reveal the depths of the play. Tragedy becomes obscure if overladen with too many conscious symbolic or psychological devices: if we set out to present *Lear* as a geriatric case history of senile dementia, the play has lost its power to move us.

Where the Conventions Merge: Black Comedy, White Tragedy

Definitions, such as "Tragedy," "Tragi-comedy," "Comedy," etc., tend to be rather misleading labels, and cannot always be applied. The prerogative of the fine dramatist is to tell a story as his imagination unfolds it, and to include the many events, sad, grand, moving, comic or pathetic that may occur. Much comedy is present in plays of tragic implication and consequences, not merely to lighten the tension and afford momentary relief. *The Revengers' Tragedy*, thought to be the work of Tourneur, continuously makes use of scandalous comedy, yet is not a satire on the "Revenge" genre. The events of this play, the corrupt humanity, the appalling fate of most of its principal characters, are presented sardonically: a grinning stoic is telling us an atrocious tale, and defying us to be sentimental about it. It defies solemn psychological motivations: indeed, one must understand what makes Lussurioso tick: his most striking characteristic is that he's a do-or-die sexual maniac, but he is written as a titanic comic monster. His blood brother, in another play of the same period, is the lycanthropic Ferdinand in Webster's *The Duchess of Malfi*: the difference in style and interpretation is that whilst Webster has regarded his subject with awe and horror, and has been sensitive to Ferdinand's tragic grandeur, Tourneur has seen Lussurioso as a figure of fun, a dangerous sideshow. Much of the subtlety of interpretation depends on our understanding the dramatist's attitude to his characters and their world. Of all great dramatists, probably only Shaw has set out to resolve our doubts about the people in his plays, and help us to share his view of them, by describing them at length.

Tourneur's métier might be described as Black Comedy, his characters, with the exception of Vindice, as puppets of villainy or virtue, types rather than people, as their names would indicate (Castiza, or chastity, naturally a woman of impregnable virtue, or Lussurioso, lust or luxury.) The play has a fearsome, garish vitality, a superhuman energy, and something of the quality of a vivid cartoon.

Yet tragedy calls above all for the most profound emotional response: the "pièce noire" affects us by shocking us, by taking an irreverent attitude to sacred matters, treating the deepest and most serious acts and motives with callous frivolity, as for example, the peripatetic corpse in Joe Orton's *Loot*. One might describe such dramatists' attitude to tragic events as that of the born survivors: they will never transcend themselves, but they will live on, understand, and endure without crying out. Tragedy, in its purest and simplest form, seems to depend on two elements: utter truthfulness of psychology, revelation of the darker side of man, and images of an unattainable beauty and perfection, the contrast between Heaven and Hell. In comedy, life is revealed: in tragedy, man.

10
Breaking the Bounds:
An Experimental Play

Every director in the theatre who owes some of his success and enjoyment to the theatre of past ages also owes something to the future. Experiment and adventure is the life-blood of the art, its renewal, and many great dramatists of the past who are accepted now as pillars of orthodoxy have been daring innovators: Chekhov, Ibsen, and Shaw were reviled in their lifetime for their choice of subject matter, or the naturalism, reality and apparent un-theatricality of their means of dramatic expression. In recent years, Robert Bolt has said that *A Man for All Seasons* owes its dramatic form to Brecht; English acting, and the psychological and physical techniques employed owe much to Stanislavsky. Craig and Appia's concepts of design and lighting have exerted a world-wide influence on scenery, the use of light and shadow, and theatre buildings. The object of all experiment, whether it has had a long-lasting influence or has been merely transitory, has been to make a better, deeper communication, to extend the boundaries of dramatic experience. Experiment has always produced a volume of appalled criticism from the public and exponents of the theatre alike, who little realize how much of their present enjoyment they owe to the courage and visionary imagination of writers and practitioners of the past. Experiment must be motivated by the desire to add to our knowledge and understanding, and has the right to fail, or achieve only qualified success; it can seldom illuminate the path to the theatre of the future, and reveal all our previous errors. Naturally in the process of exploring alternatives to conventional theatre there is prodigious waste of time and energy, and a lot of alienation of the conservatively-minded, who believe that theatricals should always follow Dr Johnson's dictum "The drama's laws the drama's patrons give, and those who live to please should please to live."

On any artist's workshop floor is a litter of incomplete work, the debris of success: the merest sketch by an artist of a previous age is venerated as giving an insight into his creative process, and perhaps as a work of art in its own right, and his integrity is never called into question because of failure to complete the work, or produce perfection.

Experiment: Why and How?

Experimental theatre so far this century has moved in three directions, basically. The first, to be more didactic, to say more, and have it understood; the next, to find more seductive forms, to intensify the emotional, as opposed to the intellectual response to theatre; and the last, to take the intellectual and emotional initiative from the audience, to prevent them from seeing a theatrical experience and turning it into what they wish to see. This invariably means that the performance will be disturbing, shocking. *Ghosts* was referred to as "an open sewer," and now seems to most sophisticated people to be genteely euphemistic in its treatment of venereal disease as a metaphor for corrupt inheritance. Blandness is a senility of theatre, and to be urgent, to be honest, may mean crying aloud for a remedy, or exposing wounds; other literature and painting have never shrunk from terrifying statements about man's ills. It may be argued that the theatre breaks a trust with the public if it affronts them: this would seem to assume two things, that conscience is only exercised in privacy, and that the relationship of the artist to the public is that of the successful whore, to entertain in exchange for money.

What place has the comic experience in adventures in theatre? Wit and ridicule, satire and exaggeration have always been used as weapons against chaos: their distortion of proportion has always sought to reveal the true proportion, the true balance. Comedy is used in two ways: to examine and expose the fallacy of verbal communication as a means of conveying thought: the school of the Absurdists, from Ionesco to N. F. Simpson have by the expression of illogicality in word and thought demonstrated that we can become the playthings of words and accepted ideas: our morality is the axiom and our inspiration the cliché. Comedy was always a sure-fire way of getting into the good books of an audience, so by an irreverent approach to art and life we may say daring and outrageous things. This is an old and time-honoured practice: the Shakespearian fool is often the man with the most pertinent things to say, licensed to do so by his capacity to clown, wrapping his pills in sugar. Comedy cuts corners, humour is for mankind, international: it can transcend both class and intellectual status.

One Adventure in Form and Content. "Interview"

Because there is no prescription for experiment, only a motive, let us examine an experimental play, and the means whereby it may be made to live on the stage. The play is *Interview*,[1] by Jean-Claude van Itallie, one of a collection of acutely socially conscious plays under the general title "America Hurrah," which emerged from the American avant-garde theatre, and which was given a wonderfully dynamic performance by the Café La Mama troupe. The play consists of two main sequences, the first, a Kafkaesque interrogation in a city employment agency, with several job-hunters being interviewed at once, the second half of the play being a series of agonized monologues by the applicants, interspersed with bizarre scenes of contemporary life—the street, the commercial gymnasium, the political meeting. The play is an acted nightmare, a whirling surrealist succession of images of the horrors and fears of modern life: the bogies are familiar—, loneliness, overwork, boredom, fear and neurosis, physical crack-up, lack of faith, in fact total alienation from the environment and society. The villains are greedy psychiatrists, moribund religion, apathetic doctors, sales campaigners and politicians. The targets of the play may be familiar, but the means chosen to shock and inform us are dazzlingly inventive. It is an experience of chaos and fear, its characters are victims and predators, and the audience's experience is through the eyes of the victims: the play is not, however, of unrelieved gloom and sombreness: it uses much humour, and its shock effect is stimulating. The quality of much of the dramatic experience is real, without being literal; the play is written for an ensemble of versatile actors, and it flows easily from scene to scene without use of scenery, the stage

[1] The passages following are quoted by permission from *Interview*, printed in *American Hurrah and other Plays* by Jean-Claude van Itallie, published by Penguin, © Jean-Claude van Itallie, 1966.

directions being "the set is white and impersonal," and the successful transition from one scene to another depends on the actors' ability to drop a character instantly and assume another, according to the demands of the scene, also their ability to make effects collectively: to represent not only people, but machines and things, and people in various stages of dehumanization. The essence of the experiment is in its ruthless use of form, verbal and dramatic.

Experiments with Tempo

Rhythm is of the utmost importance in shaping the dialogue, to produce an intentionally hypnotic effect, and is used in varied ways, together with music and dance movements:

FIRST INTERVIEWER. (*Pointing to a particular seat.*) Name, please?
FIRST APPLICANT. Jack Smith.
SECOND APPLICANT. Jane Smith.
THIRD APPLICANT. Richard Smith.
FIRST INTERVIEWER. What exactly Smith, please?
THIRD APPLICANT. Richard F.
SECOND APPLICANT. Jane Ellen.
FIRST APPLICANT. Jack none.
FIRST INTERVIEWER. What are you applying for?
FIRST APPLICANT. Housepainter.
SECOND APPLICANT. I need money.
THIRD APPLICANT. Bank president.
FIRST INTERVIEWER. How many years have you been in your present job?
THIRD APPLICANT. Three.
SECOND APPLICANT. Twenty.
FIRST APPLICANT. Eight.

The play is described as "a fugue for eight actors" and its musical effects should be exploited, as in the rhythmic, sing-song replies in the example above: the pattern of speech treated naturalistically does not produce the machine-like questions and responses, often asked, often answered. Or the droning impersonality of:

FIRST INTERVIEWER. Do you
SECOND INTERVIEWER. speak any

THIRD INTERVIEWER.	foreign
FOURTH INTERVIEWER.	languages?
FIRST INTERVIEWER.	Have you
SECOND INTERVIEWER.	got a
THIRD INTERVIEWER.	college
FOURTH INTERVIEWER.	education?

Apparently a very Lewis-Carollish conversation; the object of the stylization of speech is to turn the process of human exchange into something like a conveyor belt. In the speech above, the actors must make between them one voice, one pattern of inflection. Naturalism of action is only possible within the limits of a circumscribed world: the man on the conveyor belt may adjust his tie, the woman rummage in her purse, but the belt moves on, the characters sit and stand like Jack-in-the-boxes. So the all-pervasive rhythms, the precision of grouping and movements, is like the current of a river: it is the metaphor of consuming society, hurtling on.

Alienation or Association?

Every group of actors and director may make their own choices of action and mode of speech that will help to make meaning convey itself most forcefully. Actors spend their working lives trying to invest clichés and familiar figures of speech with spontaneity and freshness: here, perhaps, the familiar is meant to be hugely inflated, its lack of meaning strongly signalled:

ALL INTERVIEWERS.	(*In loud raucous voices.*) DO YOU SMOKE?
FIRST APPLICANT.	No thanks.
SECOND APPLICANT.	Not now.
THIRD APPLICANT.	No thanks.
FOURTH APPLICANT.	Not now.
ALL INTERVIEWERS.	(*Again in a harsh voice, bowing or courtseying.*) DO YOU MIND IF I DO?
. . . . (*Interviewers form a little group off to themselves*).	
FIRST INTERVIEWER.	I tried to quit, but couldn't manage.
SECOND INTERVIEWER.	I'm a three pack a day man, I guess.
THIRD INTERVIEWER.	If I'm gonna go I'd rather go smoking.
FOURTH INTERVIEWER.	I'm down to five a day.

Either this tiny scene can be left to work purely on the strength of its dialogue, or it can be directed to heighten its effect: in rehearsal the actors mimed the action of repeatedly drawing on their cigarettes, flourishing the cigarette, and when not actually saying their line of dialogue, repeating PuffPuffPuffPuffPuff-PuffPuff as a counterpoint to the dialogue: this little inconspicuous, but important dramatic moment has much more force and energy than if played as a purely naturalistic fragment of dialogue. It seems corny, but it worked! The play seems to alternate from devices of complete estrangement, that is putting words, meanings, and feelings into a totally bizarre and alien context, to supportive and imitative actions, where the other actors mime and make sounds which contribute to the explanation of atmosphere and meaning. Many of the alienation devices seem random and arbitrary: much sophistry goes into explaining away the random happenings that occur in experiments in theatre. Some symbols cannot be explained, but seem justified, because, like the paintings of Magritte, "Who would have thought it?" A picture does not carry on its frame ten closely written lines of explanation, it conveys its message wordlessly: so should the acted devices used to enhance the implications of this play.

Consider this example: each candidate has just been interrogated about his probity and political neutrality:

(Applicants and Interviewers line up for a square dance. Music under the following.)

FIRST APPLICANT.   *(Bowing to first interviewers.)* What's it to you, buddy?

SECOND APPLICANT.   *(Bowing to second interviewer.)* Eleanor Roosevelt wasn't more honest.

THIRD APPLICANT.   *(Bowing to third interviewer.)* My record is lily white, sir!

FOURTH APPLICANT.   *(Bowing to fourth interviewer.)* Mrs Thumbletwat used to take me to the bank and I'd watch her open her box!

The characters mince and prance with absurd formality during this little exchange: instead of it being just so much superfluous dialogue, the audience sits up and takes notice: we are all constrained to be polite, to smile and be correct in circumstances which are unpleasant.

The Assault on the Emotions

People are being lived, rather than living: some external agency, some force tosses the characters about: they are all frantically trying to move with the speed and energy of this external force: sometimes they suceed, at other times they, and the world, are hopelessly at odds:

(Music under: the characters stop and freeze. The second interviewer, acting as policeman, begins to line them up in a diagonal line, like marching dolls, one behind the other. As they are put in line they begin to move their mouths without sound, like fish in a tank. The music stops.)

SECOND INTERVIEWER.	My
FOURTH APPLICANT.	fault.
SECOND APPLICANT.	Excuse
FOURTH INTERVIEWER.	me.
FIRST INTERVIEWER.	Can you
SECOND APPLICANT.	help
FIRST APPLICANT.	me?
FOURTH INTERVIEWER.	Next.

By now the line of actors is marching toward the audience, yet not advancing: their movement becomes more strenuous, their expression more agonized, they are beginning to shout: the scene rises to a crescendo of blackening, screaming figures as the lights fade slowly on them: there is no answer to their pleas, their apologies:

SECOND INTERVIEWER.	My
FOURTH APPLICANT.	fault.
SECOND APPLICANT.	EXCUSE
FOURTH INTERVIEWER.	ME!
FIRST INTERVIEWER.	...CAN...YOU...
SECOND APPLICANT.	...HELP...
FIRST APPLICANT.	...ME!!
FOURTH INTERVIEWER.	NEXT....

The humans have surrendered. They have turned into robot-like, grisly figures.

The violent monologues use a variety of techniques as a vivid background to the sufferings of the characters: a harassed, garrulous telephonist spills out her anxieties about C.A.N.C.E.R., her bellyache, yesterday's glutinous lunch, to the accompaniment of an inhuman background of a telephone exchange, created by the other actors: they move like the parts of a machine, they ring, distort, crackle, buzz, hum, voices and conversations cross over and merge. A girl, tense and crazed, enters a party: the man she was coming with has suffered a hideous street accident: she must tell somebody:

> ... so I said his arm was torn out of its socket and his face was on the pavement gasping, BUT I DIDN'T TOUCH HIM and she smiled and walked away and I said after her you aren't supposed to touch someone before——I WANTED TO HELP, I said, but she wasn't listening when a man came up and said was it someone you knew and I said YES it was someone I knew slightly someone I knew, YES, and he offered me a drink and I said no thanks I didn't want one and he said well how well did I know him and I said I knew him well, Yes, I KNEW HIM VERY WELL. . . .

In the background, on another plane, the party is taking place: people drink, smile, converse, eat peanuts and canapés, dance and letch: they talk and laugh: entirely in slow motion: that's how grotesque they look to her. The speed of all these banal and harmless actions makes them appear horrifying: all human communication is broken; a grin becomes the slow smile of an idiot, people dancing make movements which become obscene and gross, somebody pushed aside turns into a sprawl of limbs and an angry contorted mask.

Character is vividly encapsulated in short scenes, and the actors must capture its essence without the aid of costume (the play specifies that the cast should be dressed in black and white street clothes) or of dramatically plausible dialogue which justifies and explains who they are: consider the monstrous politician of the last scene of the play, who harangues his audience with platitudes, evades all important issues, and substitutes glad-handing for sincerity: an Ed Begley or George C. Scott role! As he sweet-talks, hectors, and raves, he describes himself in action, with phrases that should be delivered like asides, with a mere turn of the head to the audience:

> Thank you very much, I said cheerfully, and good luck to you,
> I said, turning my smile to the next one. . . . Our children are
> our most important asset, I agreed earnestly. Yes they are,
> I said solemnly. Children, I said, with a long pause [here the
> actor should actually hold the pause], are our most important
> asset. I only wish I could, madame, I said earnestly, standing
> tall, but rats, I said regretfully, are a city matter.

The actor must in this violent scene achieve exactly the right
note of the rasping demagogue, his glittering smile, his hypnotic
intonations, his oratorical gestures. At the end of his speech, like
a marionette, he topples slowly from his box, and like a gramo-
phone record slowing down, he starts his speech, with exactly the
same words, all over again.

Only Connect. . . .

This is a play without a story, and without dramatic time, in the
sense that episodes lead from one to the other, gradually unfolding the play and its characters. The scenes however, need
linking, or smooth transition: the emotional pitch must be sustained, as the play would seem to work by a sustained assault on
the senses: these linkages have been ingeniously contrived by the
dramatist. A scene of comedy, set in a gymnasium, uses the actors
moving in continuous rhythms: in pursuit of health, beauty, and
sexiness, a group of citizens are being exercised by a cynical in-
structor: perspiring overweight housewives, arch and sexy typists,
middle-aged men giving themselves coronaries, perform their
routine fairly ridiculously to the running commentary of a bored
he-man:

> Now ladies. AND breathe it in and stick em out and step
> right out and four. AND breathe it in and stick them out. Stick
> them OUT! That's what you got them for, isn't it? I told
> them. And keep it nice, all of you. You're SELLING. Selling
> all the time. That's right, isn't it Miss? Right, I said. . . . And
> breathe it in and stick it out, step right out and smile. And
> breathe it in and stick it out and step right out and SMILE. . . .

The regular movement of the actors, a rhythm of three beats, gets
faster and faster, their movement smaller and smaller, until it

changes to the shaking vibration of passengers in a subway train: one actress, exhausted, falls out, and sits panting on one of the boxes on the stage, turning into the beat-up and defeated char-woman of the next scene: two more actors take Mr Universe posture on two more boxes, turning into figures in advertisements, jockey shorts, dry-shavers, or something similar, and the instruc-tor's chant gradually turns into da-da-da, da-da-da, of the train's wheels. The pantings of the gymnasts turns into the hiss of brakes and doors of a subway train. The examples shown here are merely one approach to this clever and ferocious play, an attempt to understand its handling of dramatic form, and the way in which an audience might respond to it.

Berkoff's Theatre

Berkoff's intention: "To express drama in the most vital way imaginable; to perform at the height of one's power with all available means." The three directors/creators who have probably had the greatest effect on English theatre in the last two decades are Peter Brook, Joan Littlewood, and Steven Berkoff. If three artists so different could be said to have one common aim, it is to create a *popular* theatre, enjoyed and understood by the largest number and widest selection of people. The prospect of playing to empty houses concentrates the mind wonderfully, so these three have devoted immense thought and work to the nature of the theatre experience: what it consists of, how it's done, and who it's for. Briefly, Brook has sought to make it a simpler experience, more direct, to strip from the play what he deems to be unnecessary orna-mentation, mere show and irrelevant excitements, and fal-lals, on the premise that the convincing emotional part of the experience may be lost or obscured under a welter of trivia. Littlewood's aim has appeared to be to drag the play away from the preoccupation with middle-class life, thought and crises with which the commercial theatre busied itself for decades, and expand the theatre to embrace, with depth and compassion, the lives and thoughts of ordinary working people. Both have been powerful guiding forces to actors, writers, directors and designers.

Berkoff has either from choice or necessity had to be his own author, impresario, director, and more often than not, leading actor. This sweat and solitude has produced a remarkable vitality and originality both in choice of material, and the nature of the actor's performance. He has taken a fresh view of great works (*Agamemnon*, *Metamorphosis*, *The Fall of The House of Usher*), and created powerful, funny and moving new works in *East* and *Decadence*. As an actor, director, and mime (and brave eclectic) he has sought, and often found, a deepening of the actor's possible skills. First, let him explain himself:

> Imagination is the great rambling whale of the audience's mind that must be harpooned by the controlled imagination from the stage . . . it must be hooked, trapped, and made one hy the hypnotic power of the performers and their gestures . . . the spirit of magic and fairytale should pervade the stage. . . .

> By leaving space for the spectator, by eliminating the junk of sets and over-explained narrative the spectator can become part of it and is linked to the events by the demands of his imagination that is interpreting for itself what is happening.

> In searching for material for these plays, I found the finished play too finite a form, simply a mass of dialogue, with no resonances of inner life, where the actors hurled situational chat at each other.

Clearly, having made such brave declarations, he must make the plays work, and prove his point; so what do the plays contain, and what are the means? What is different, and how does he propose to heighten and intensify the experience? First, the visual emphasis is on the actor, his body, its shape and its actions. I offered on p. 71 the idea that the actor and director could draw inspiration from everything they see, from life, art, music, natural things and made things, behaviour, customs, and so on. Berkoff produces a great number of powerful images, which one would think to be unactable, except to a mime, whose sole purpose is to create the tangible world without any visible assistance from it. From *East*:

All quotations of text, Berkoff's commentary, and his declarations of intent from Playscript 78, *East, Agammemnon, The Fall of the House of Usher*, Steven Berkoff, Pub. John Calder.

Mike turns Les into a motor bike and jumps on his back,
using Les's arms as handlebars. The two clearly create the
sound of a motor bike revving up and changing gear. . . .
The strength of the machine and the movement as it careers
round corners should be apparent.

The homecoming of the triumphant Agamemnon is staged
by the actors as a troop of horses; they must play both the
horse and the rider. It's a very exciting scene. The horses/
horsemen walk, trot, canter, and gallop, pell-mell: they
whisper, utter, sing, and bellow only one word, AGAMEM-
NON! Till it becomes a continuous thunder. They whip and
flay their horses and each other. The event builds relentlessly
to an overwhelming outburst of power and energy—the
dramatist says "It still goes on". It reaches a climax and
gradually slows down, reined back with the *uttermost effort* and
shimmers into a grand and stately entrance, ending with an
impressive, silent stillness: a frozen frame, a breathtaking
moment. Berkoff, like Shaw, intends his stage directions for
posterity: "Chorus members may die in this enactment, and
must not take part unless they have strong hearts"—like GBS,
with tongue in cheek. *The Fall of The House of Usher* builds up
to the horrific entombment of Madeline Usher. The play is a
surreal scenario, using filmic time, cuts, juxtapositions and
effects. Berkoff accompanies his spare text with a commentary
and description:

SCENE 27.	Madeline has slipped behind a gauze curtain. Lights up on her waking in coffin. She mimes pounding and scratching on coffin lid, struggling to escape. BLACKOUT.
(COMMENTARY).	She mimes the solid confines with her hands, tries to claw at the sides of her tomb . . . The harp transmits the terrible and awful scratching.
SCENE 29.	Usher stops pacing. He listens. Listens. SCREAMS. LIGHTS UP ON MADELINE IN COFFIN. TAPE OF POUNDING WITH NINE SCREAMS. She struggles to escape.

(COMMENTARY).   Madeline demented and pounding on the coffin
accompanied by the most horrific screams rending
through the theatre—screams almost inhuman—
her light, sulphurous, murky and deadly . . . their
fearful sound, the sounds of animals having their
entrails torn out. . . .

A dreadful scene. In Berkoff's production the striking effect
was Madeline's hands, shredded, bloody claws.

Just three examples of many. As evocative, or stirring as a
painting, a beautiful place, a scorpion, a steak, a Boeing 747, a
corpse. Their aim is a tremendous and vivid reality, which is
not literal, not photographic: it is to create a reality engen-
dered of emotions. The actor alone is the total instrument.

Berkoff has a refreshing approach to language, arrived at by
experience and instinct and the desire to make his meaning
plain but rich. Quite often Berkoff leaves the actor to punctuate and phrase a speech for himself. His plays are full of
brawny imagery, and cannot be considered in terms of conventional propriety or as precise philosophical, moral or intellectual statements. He is often verbally violent and obscene, but
never gratuitously so, and enjoys the lyrical and evocative:

CLYTEMNESTRA.   A whiplash of lightening like molten gold/the
sharks danced to see the beacons glow/each
sleepy watchman fired his sticks in turn/so a current of flame streaked over Euripus/hill to hill/
crackle scorch and burn/it soared it swung it
came/like an avenging angel across a frozen
forest of stars . . .

The steaming, dreaming, yearning world of *East* is evoked in
language which combines reality with poetry, the colour and
smack of slang and the demotic with Shakespearean grandeur:

MIKE.   He clocked the bird I happened to be fianced to, my
darling Sylv (of legendary knockers) and I doth take it
double strong that this long git in suede and rubber,
pimples sprouting forth like buttercups on sunny days
from off his greasy boat: that he should dare to lay upon
her svelte and tidy form his horror leering jellies . . .

SYLV.   She were in ingredients of flesh pack suavely fresh . . .
deodorised and knicker-white . . . lip gleam and teethed . . .
Piss off, thou lump . . .

MIKE.   I'll chart thy surfaces until thou criest from within thy
depths. . . .

Berkoff is after what the mind and soul are shouting, not our
circumspect croakings that pass for human intercourse. The
compelling fever of talk doesn't let up, any more than it does in
MacBeth.

Usher is much more sparing of language, perhaps because it
is so vivid in visual imagery. Berkoff: "What we attempted in
the following play was a grotesque, surreal, paranoiac view of
life such as is conjured up in dreams."

Servant leaves: Usher transforms into house. Usher begins singing
her name as he approaches. Madeline always intertwined like ivy
or fungi with Usher becomes the pen writing . . . The Friend and
Madeline are sculpted into seated positions on non-existent
chairs. She becomes a stringed instrument which he plays.

USHER.   I shall perish,
I must perish
Thus, thus and not otherwise
Shall I be lost.

and:

FRIEND.   The days pass one by one.
Her name is not mentioned
I try to drown my mind in
Roderick's strange music.

and:

USHER AND FRIEND.   Vaults
Long unopened
Oppressive
Smell
Damp
lightless
remote
Stinking

There is enormous variety within these plays: the rules of logic, everyday realith, gravity, decorum, Actor's Equity, and The Ancient Order of Buffaloes are continually broken. Yet the consequences are always understandable, compellingly involving, moving and funny. To the depths of one's being.

Directors and actors must seek constantly for new means, new material: the stuff of experimental theatre is undiscovered metaphors, deeper revelation of human possibility, dissolving of meaningless conventions and taboos. This attitude should co-exist with a knowledge of, and respect for theatrical orthodoxy: nor should adventurous actors and directors be discouraged by the fact that someone at some time has made the same experiments, with great success or disastrously. Everybody who works sincerely and thoughtfully in the theatre adds something, however small, to the art: theatre is for man, not man for theatre: through it he expresses his humanity, his thought, and his identity.

Conclusions:
The Director's Progress

The director should never stop learning. His schools are theory and practice. The varied techniques of acting, speech, movement, interpretation, design and theatre technology, have been written about extensively by specialists, who have tried to set down the sum of their knowledge and experience. Their books should be read and enjoyed. The first test of the director's balance, his creativeness, is his willingness to learn, to try to understand other people's creative process, and their skills. He must know how to solve the actor's problems on a fundamental level: audibility, meaning, the use of the emotions to produce truthful acting, repose, economy and expressiveness of movement, and if he lacks knowledge or intuition in any area of the actor's craft he must study and experiment to understand it. The actor must believe that the director is sincere in his approach to interpretation, and have implicit faith in his technical advice. Being only human, the director will make mistakes, change his ideas, and often fail to see the right way to achieve an end: if the actor believes in the director, he will gladly suffer with him, in fact he will help him to solve the problem. The personal relationship between actors and director is probably the most important single factor in useful direction, given that the director has enthusiasm, knowledge of acting, and discernment. Every director has to find out, by a painful process, his or her effect on people, just as the actor must: and self-discipline must be exercised to get results. A good-natured and sensitive director may suffer from actors indulging themselves: he must learn to be firm, severe if necessary, and the pursuit of artistic truth is his guide: equally, a director of strong ideas and convictions must learn to bend, to be receptive, or a serious-minded and rather intense director must acquire the art of being pleasant, especially in rehearsals of comedies. Quite simply, they must want to work hard for you. Directing is something of a performance, but a director cannot afford tantrums, and must never be out of control: this may mean a valiant display of pleasure at an indifferent rehearsal, or deliberately being demanding or critical to produce the right response.

The actor if talented is a moody, volatile, mercurial person, and a word can crush him, or release something fruitful and creative. Finding the right thing to say is a matter of sensitivity and flair: in a delightful production of *Scapin* at the Young Vic, Frank Dunlop gave Job Stewart, playing an incensed father, the instruction "play it SITTING DOWN." The result of this apparently obscure and impossible instruction was a characterization which was wildly funny, a chalk-stripe-suited, homburg-hatted, umbrella-toting figure, who loped about like Groucho Marx with bent knees, a furious arthritic dwarf, but utterly credible. Being able to talk to actors does not mean garrulity, or dazzling them and overwhelming them with ideas and instructions, however right: it simply means saying the right thing at the right time.

A talent for casting is vital, and is a highly developed instinct. Casting should never be done by committee, a common practice in the amateur theatre, presumably to ensure fair shares for all, but is the sole responsibility of the director. If an amateur company wishes to make the fullest use of its actors, and develop the younger or less experienced, it must choose plays that offer the right parts. Auditioning must be thorough, in all circumstances: the director only offers an actor a role if he is very familiar with his work, sure of his skill, and knows how he or she responds to rehearsal: even then, diplomatic preliminary discussions should take place to find out the actor's attitude to the part. It may be so different from the director's that it would be impossible for them to amalgamate their ideas. It is customary to ask the actor to prepare and present two short, different speeches, to give an indication of range, and perhaps to ask him to improvise: if the technique of reading a scene is used, the actor must have time to read and roughly comprehend the play in advance, and the director should make this reading into a miniature rehearsal, to help the actor toward giving a better reading: a lot may be revealed by saying "Very good/interesting/fascinating, now will you read the scene again as if she were a fussier/ more ironic/ sillier/ more contented sort of person." Never cast by competitive readings, with all the aspirant actors sitting round a table: do it in private. The qualities to look for are repose: an actor walks steadily to the centre of the stage, and those few seconds reveal a lot about his poise, posture, body control, shape and looks. He speaks: tone, variety of volume, and pitch, clarity of articulation and interpretative ideas can be discerned in a dozen lines of dialogue. If he dries a lot, he's got poor concentration, or is lazy or given to panic, but allowance must be made for the fact that the actor will be nervous, and may croak and tremble for a few moments, or that the actor may have made a bad choice of speech. Fussiness, producing props, a great deal of movement and business, emoting, all indicate an actor who is naïve or lacking in judgement, mistaking all these shallow things for a true demonstration of acting ability. The exhibitionist actor, the actor who is badly adjusted in his personality, must be avoided: he will consume the time and attention of the director and the other actors. It there is any doubt about the actor's capacity for working with people, don't cast him: or if you do cast a notoriously difficult actor, make sure he is worth the pains! Bear in mind that some actors are deemed "difficult" because they are dogmatic, or very sure of themselves, or have told a foolish and under-talented director to go and jump in the lake.

Training for Directors

For the would-be director, or the young director with some experience who wants further training in the skills and practice of directing, there is a certain amount of professional training available. To enter any of these courses requires motivation, time, money, and strong evidence of some previous suitable experience in acting, directing, or any other theatre arts. The competition for courses at any reputable establishment is considerable, and the aims and standards of the courses correspondingly high. Many students receive grants. For the young adult student, three of the recognized Drama Schools offer director training: the East 15 Acting School runs a three-year course, the Bristol Old Vic Theatre School and The Drama

Studio each have a one-year course. The National Council of
Drama Training is currently surveying the field of director
training opportunities. A number of Regional Education
Authorities provide some degree of director training, and
should be contacted for information. The British Theatre
Association at 9 Fitzroy Square, London W1 runs a twice-
yearly ten week full-time course for directors, and awards a
certificate to successful students. For the more experienced
young director, the Arts Council of Great Britain runs a
director's training scheme, in which its trainees are attached to
a theatre and its directorate to gain further experience on a
high professional level. The Independent Broadcasting Association run a similar scheme. For both these latter schemes there
is tremendous competition, and a high degree of promise or
achievement is required.

Directing is very hard work, and mental stamina is vital. No
moment of rehearsal with the director present should escape his
concentration; he must pay attention to every detail, every nuance
of meaning and feeling. The development of a play arises not
from his preconceived ideas, but from pursuing the faint bleep-
bleeps that occur in rehearsal. Knowing when to interrupt the
actor is an art, a touch that can only develop with experience,
as is knowing when to leave the actor alone. A good actor can
only resolve certain problems on his own, two actors playing a
scene together may need each other more than they need the
director, and at times a whole company of actors may be mentally
signalling "just let us get on with it." Rehearsals must be made
interesting and purposeful for the actors and staff, and this means
good use of people's time, a spirit of search and inquiry, and
always a spirit of optimism and belief that the play is worth
while, that the actors will, finally, surpass themselves and that
the audience will enjoy, or be moved by, the play. It might be
thought that a busy director has little time to watch the world
wag, but every good director must find room in his life for
observing mankind: theatre is not about actors and actresses,
directors and designers, technicians and stage hands, or even the
opinions and convictions of dramatists: it is about life, human
thought and feeling, human experience.

Actors, directors and audiences alike lament the lack of "something new." This is comparable to demanding the rebuilding of St Peter's, or the demolition of Venice; instead, let new cities, new cathedrals grow beside the old, and let the old and the new be sumptuously decorated. To the actor in search of a role, the director in search of a play, the audience in search of laughter or wisdom, these writers, among many others, have riches to offer:

Aristophanes. Euripides. Sophocles. Aeschylus. Marlowe. Shakespeare. Jonson. Webster. Tourneur. Molière. Vanbrugh. Farquhar. Otway. Congreve. Sheridan. Goldsmith. Garrick and Coleman. T. W. Robertson. Dion Boucicault. Ibsen. Strindberg. Chekhov. Turgenev. Wilde. Pinero. Shaw. Feydeau. Labiche. Priestley. O'Neill. Odets. Moss Hart and George S. Kauffmann. Lorca. Pirandello. Zuckmayer. Harold Brighouse. D. H. Lawrence. Brecht. James Bridie. Rattigan. T. S. Elliot. Fry. O'Casey. Ben Travers. Coward. Frederick Lonsdale. Anouilh. Wesker. Arden. Pinter. Genet. Osborne. Orton. Ionesco. Charles Wood. John Whiting. N. F. Simpson. Arthur Miller. Tennessee Williams. Edward Albee. J. P. Donleavy. Peter Shaffer. Henry Livings. Dürrenmatt. Hochhuth. Henri de Montherlant. Peter Weiss. Neil Simon. Arthur Kopit. Samuel Beckett. John Spurling. Edward Bond. Tom Stoppard. Sam Shepherd. Christopher Hampton. James Saunders. Marguerite Duras. Robert Bolt. Willy Russell.

Thinking of these names, and their work, is where directing begins. Understanding actors is where directing goes on.

Bibliography

Direction, Production Theory, and Theatre History

Some of these books are no longer in print but might still be available from libraries.

A Sense of Direction. John Fernald: Secker and Warburg, London 1968

The Empty Space. Peter Brook: McGibbon and Kee, London/ Penguin, Harmondsworth, Middlesex

Directing a Play. James Roose-Evans: Studio Vista, London

Experimental Theatre. James Roose-Evans: Studio Vista, London 1970

Theatre in the Round. Stephen Joseph: Barrie and Rockcliffe, London

A Life in the Theatre. Tyrone Guthrie: Hamish Hamilton, London 1960; McGraw-Hill, New York 1959

On the Art of the Theatre. Gordon Craig: Heinemann, London 1968

Stage Directions. John Gielgud: Heinemann, London 1963

The Theatre and its Double. Antonin Artaud: Grove Press, New York 1958

Brecht: A Choice of Evils. Martin Esslin: Heinemann, London

Shakespeare Our Contemporary. Jan Kott: Heinemann. London 1967

Theatre of the Absurd: Martin Esslin, Heinemann, London

The Development of the Theatre. Allardyce Nicholl: Harrap, London 1966

The Director and the Stage. Edward Braun: Methuen, London

Play Directing. Francis Hodge: Prentice Hall, New York

On Directing. Harold Clurman: Collier/Macmillan, New York

Directing Drama. John Miles-Brown: Peter Owen, London

First Reading to First Night. Malcolm Black: University of Washington Press, Seattle

World Theatre. Bamber Gascoigne: Michael Joseph, London

My Life in Art. Stanislavsky: Bles, London; Little Brown and Co., New York

The Improvised Play, Paul Clements: Methuen

Theatre Games, Clive Barker: Methuen

Direction by Indirection, Michael L. Greenwald: University Press of Delaware

Prospero's Staff, Charles Merowitz: Indiana Press
Directors on Directing, Toby Cole and Helen Krich Chinoy: Macmillan
Great Directors at Work, David Richard Jones: California Press
Community Plays, Anne Jellicoe: Methuen
Play Direction, John E. Dietrich and Ralph W. Duckwall: Prentice Hall
Getting the Show On: Musicals, Lehman Engel: Shirmer Books
Directing a Play, Michael McCaffery: Phaidon
A Sense of Direction, William Gaskill: Faber & Faber
Subsequent Performances, Jonathan Miller: Faber and Faber

Acting and Acting Skills

Tyrone Guthrie on Acting: Studio Vista, London 1971
Theatre. The Rediscovery of Style. Michel St Denis: Heinemann, London 1960
The Actor's Ways and Means. Michael Redgrave: Heinemann, London 1966
The Craft of Comedy. Haggard and Seyler: Miller, London
Acting in the Sixties. Hal Burton: BBC, London 1970
Building a Character. Stanislavsky: Bles, London 1968
An Actor Prepares. Stanislavsky: Bles, London 1937; Theatre Arts Inc., New York
Creating a Role. Stanislavsky: Bles
Drama for Youth. Richard Courtney: Pitman, London
Techniques of the Stage Fight. William Hobbs: Studio Vista, London
Voice and Speech in the Theatre. J. Clifford Turner: A & C Black, London
Voice and the Actor. Cicely Berry: Harrap, London
Impro. Keith Johnstone: Methuen, London
About Acting. Peter Barkworth: Secker and Warburg, London
Clear Speech. Malcolm Morrison: A & C Black, London
The Actor and his Body. Litz Pisk: Harrap, London
Training for the Theatre. Michel Saint-Denis: Heinemann, London
The Psychology of the Actor. Yoti Lane: Greenwood Press,
Mime. Kay Hamblin: Lutterworth, Guildford
The Way of the Actor, Brian Bates: Century
The Actor and his Text, Cicely Berry: Harrap
The Alexander Principle, William Barlow: Arrow
The Use of the Self, F. M. Alexander: Gollancz
Being an Actor, Simon Callow: Penguin
So You Want to be an Actor?, Adrian Rendle: A & C Black

Ideal Voice and Speech Training, Ken Parkin: French
Actors on Acting, Toby Cole and Helen Krich Chinoy: Crown

Technical Theatre: Design, Lighting, Costume and Make-up

Stage Lighting. Richard Pilbrow: Studio Vista, London
The Art of Stage Lighting. Frederick Bentham: A & C Black, London
Staging The Play. Nora Lambourne: Studio Publications, London
Scenic Painting and Design. Stephen Joseph: Pitman, London 1964
Stage Properties and How to Make Them. W. Kenton: A & C Black,
    London
The Art of Scenic Design. Lee Simonson: Harrap, London
New Theatre Forms. Stephen Joseph: Pitman, London 1968
Practical Stage Management. R. Perrotet: Studio Vista, London
Costume in The Theatre. James Laver: Harrap, London 1964
The Cut of Women's Clothes. 1600–1930. N. Waugh: Faber, London
The Cut of Men's Clothes. 1600–1930. N. Waugh: Faber, London
The History of English Costume. Iris Brooke: Methuen, London
Stage Make Up. Richard Blore: Stacey Publications, London
Stage Makeup. Herman Buchman: Pitman, London 1972
Make-up for Theatre, Film and Television. Lee Baygan: A & C Black,
    London and Drama Book Publishers, New York
Stage Sound. David Collison: Cassell, London
Theatre Administration. Francis Reid: A & C Black, London
Designing and Painting for the Theatre. Lynn Peckfall: Holt, Rinehart
    Winston, New York
Scene Design, Stage Lighting, Sound, Costume and Make-Up. Willard
    F. Bellman: Harper and Row: New York
English Costume. Doreen Yarwood: Batsford, London
The Anatomy of Costume. Robert Selbie: Bell & Hyman, London
The Language of Clothes. Alison Lurie: Random House, New York
Creating Your Own Stage Lighting, Tim Streader and John A.
    Williams, Bell & Hyman
Who Does What in the Theatre, Judith Cook: Harrap
Stage Design and Properties, Michael Holt: Phaidon
Stage Management and Administration, Pauline Meanear and Terry
    Hawkins: Phaidon
Lighting and Sound, Neil Fraser: Phaidon
Small Stage Sets on Tour, James Hull Miller: Meriwether Publishing
    Ltd
Create Your Own Stage Sets, Terry Thomas: A & C Black
Stage Crafts, Chris Hoggett: A & C Black
Costumes for the Stage, Sheila Jackson: Herbert Press
Period Costume for Stage and Screen, Jean Hunnisett: Bell & Hyman

Index